CANNABIZ

CANNABIZ

The Explosive Rise of the
Medical Marijuana Industry

JOHN GELUARDI

PoliPointPress

14   13   12   11   10   1   2   3   4   5

Production management: BookMatters
Book design: BookMatters
Cover design: Nicole Hayward

Cover art created from RX bottle © Roel Smart;
Cannabis bud © Scott Cramer; Cannabis leaf
© Shaun Lombard

Library of Congress Cataloging-in-Publication Data

Geluardi, John.
    Cannabiz : the explosive rise of the medical
marijuana industry / John Geluardi.
        p.   cm.
    Includes bibliographical references and index.
    ISBN 978-0-9824171-9-5 (alk. paper)
    1. Marijuana—Therapeutic use—United
States—History.   2. Pharmaceutical industry—
United States—History.   I. Title.
    RM666.C266G45   2010
    338.4'761532345—dc22   2010023956

Published by:
PoliPointPress, LLC
80 Liberty Ship Way, Suite 22
Sausalito, CA 94965
(415) 339-4100
www.p3books.com
Distributed by Ingram Publisher Services
Printed in the USA

For Alix

Contents

Introduction

The seed for this book was planted in 2000, when I was a newspaper reporter in Berkeley, California. At that time, Berkeley's city council was struggling to regulate some of the nation's first medical marijuana dispensaries. Proposition 215, the California initiative that had legalized medical marijuana four years earlier, had proven to be awkward and incomplete. For example, state law allowed dispensaries to sell marijuana, but growing or transporting it remained illegal. Under federal law, of course, marijuana was still completely illegal, and federal officials had increased their enforcement efforts after the passage of Proposition 215.

My initial idea was to write a magazine story about the life of a marijuana plant from the time its seed was planted in the wilds of northern California through its harvest, shipping, and finally its sale in a Bay Area dispensary. I wanted the story to include colorful rebels and misfits living on the margins of society. But I soon discovered growers were reluctant to show me their crops, much less permit me to follow them through an entire season. Eventually the idea took a backseat to other stories and deadlines.

When I revisited the story idea nine years later, the business of marijuana had changed dramatically. The tenacious weed had grown like Jack's gold-laden beanstalk, but the gold was no fairy tale. The cannabis industry as a whole, both legal and illegal, was generating by some estimates $115 billion annually. Cottage industries were flourishing: hydroponics supply stores, construction companies specializing in grow rooms, cannabis-friendly travel agencies, and a trade school with four campuses dedicated to training cannabis industry workers and entrepreneurs. By that time, the dispensaries had developed a support network that included elected officials, attorneys, public relations firms, unions, media, and nonprofit advocacy groups, all energetically promoting the public acceptance of medical marijuana.

And popular culture reflected that new acceptance. *Weeds*, a cable television show, featured a suburban housewife selling marijuana to make ends meet. Another cable program, *Cannabis Planet TV*, presented marijuana-based news as well as cooking and cultivation tips. Dozens of magazines, newspapers, Web sites, and blogs were focusing almost entirely on marijuana. In many states, billboards and radio broadcasts advertised medical marijuana services. Harvest festivals, THC expos, and marijuana seminars were being attended by thousands of people year round, even in states that hadn't legalized medical marijuana.

Public attitudes had shifted dramatically. According to the 2009 World Drug Report, 31 million Americans had used marijuana the previous year. The corresponding number at the end of the 1960s—a few years before President Nixon launched the seemingly endless war on drugs—was 6 million. The U.S. Department of Health and Human Services reported that more than 100 million Americans had tried marijuana at least once at some point in their lifetime. Two national polls taken in 2010 showed that nearly 80 percent of Americans supported medical marijuana, and roughly 44 percent would vote for full legalization.

Despite this widespread support, the industry had its critics. Many argued that dispensaries eagerly catered to perfectly healthy people. In fact, some dispensaries were running promotions that blatantly suggested adult recreation. Their advertisements featured glossy images of glistening marijuana buds and underdressed women enveloped in tendrils of wafting smoke—more Bob Marley than Blue Cross. Also, many dispensaries marketed strains of marijuana using names like "Trainwreck," "Big Fatty," and "Cat Piss," which did not sound remotely medicinal. And though medical marijuana laws required a doctor's written recommendation (federal law prohibited prescriptions) to purchase pot, obtaining one was embarrassingly easy. In California, all it took was a few minutes, a couple hundred bucks, and a little imagination. Casual observation at a typical dispensary indicated a high percentage of patients were American males between the ages of 18 and 35—one of the healthiest demographic groups on the planet.

The bar was so low for obtaining a medical marijuana recommendation that it had become something of a joke. In a comedic scene of the HBO series *Entourage*, Kevin Dillon, who plays a television character actor, visits an evaluation clinic for a recommendation. But worried that whatever illness he claims might damage his virile public image, he and the doctor bandy possible ailments until they settle on a suitable anxiety disorder.

But criticism hadn't slowed the industry's growth, which the business community has begun to track. A September 2009 feature in *Fortune* magazine entitled "How Marijuana Became

Legal" compared the growth of the medical marijuana industry to that of gambling. Initially gambling was legal only in Nevada. After New Jersey legalized it, other states followed; now almost every state in the union allows gaming. The article described the professionalism that some California dispensaries were practicing and attempted to estimate the size of the state's medical marijuana market. The actual numbers are frustratingly elusive because the California Board of Equalization, which oversees state sales taxes, does not keep separate tax information on medical marijuana dispensaries. However, the article assigned an average revenue of $3 million to $4 million to each of the state's estimated 700 dispensaries—the actual number of dispensaries is probably much higher—and reasoned that medical marijuana was generating roughly $220 million in sales tax. That figure did not include federal employee–payroll taxes paid by dispensary employees.

Harvard economist Jeffrey Miron calculated potential tax revenue if marijuana were legalized throughout the United States. According to his 2010 study, state and federal governments would save $13.7 billion in law enforcement costs. Assuming legalization would hurt value, Miron put the national market at $14 billion. On the basis of that figure, Miron estimated federal and state revenues, including various excise and sin taxes, would be $6.7 billion.

Miron's critics argued his estimates were low, and others estimated the national market to be roughly $120 billion, but the most commonly cited estimates fall between $35 billion and $45 billion.[1]

With that kind of money being made in a bad economy, there occurred a "green rush" to get in on the ground floor of a new and profitable industry. Young entrepreneurs with newly minted business degrees were quickly replacing the counterculture pioneers, outlaws, and rebels of a generation ago. The industry was recruiting open-faced members of the Students for Sensible Drug Policy, a college organization with chapters on more than 200 campuses nationwide.

This book begins with a look at this burgeoning industry, its history, and its prospects. Chapter two recounts the everyday medical use of cannabis in the nineteenth century, its recreational use in the early twentieth century, the government's aggressive campaign to demonize it in the 1930s, and its federal prohibition in 1937. Chapter three tracks marijuana's slow return to a place in the public's esteem, its emergence from the shadows with the 1996 passage of Proposition 215 in California, and other states' decisions to permit medical marijuana despite opposition from law enforcement agencies.

The next few chapters present current efforts to regulate the new industry in the face of considerable confusion and instability. In California, that state of flux has led to remarkably different local ordinances. Cities like Oakland, for example, successfully regulated the medical marijuana industry while others, like Los Angeles, fell into chaos.

Chapter six profiles professionals now working in the industry and their efforts to shape the cultivation and sale of medical marijuana into traditional business models, complete with recommended best practices, trade associations, and advisory councils. The industry has begun to attract college graduates who are not only eager to be a part of what they regard as an exciting new enterprise, but who also view full legalization as comparable to the civil rights movement of the 1950s and 1960s.

Chapter seven focuses on the responses of politicians, many of whom have been reluctant to support the industry openly for fear of political backlash. But that is slowly changing. A new breed of politician is embracing the medical marijuana industry as a valid source of local tax revenue and job creation.

As the industry has grown in stature, power, and popularity, so has talk of taking the next step—full legalization of adult use, which is the topic of chapter eight. Industry leaders are in sharp disagreement over when and how that campaign should begin. Even so, a legalization initiative made the 2010 ballot in California, and three other states shepherded similar initiatives. The state efforts caused legalization advocacy groups, such as the National Organization for the Reform of Marijuana Laws (NORML) and the Marijuana Policy Project, to shift a greater portion of their attention from lobbying in Washington, DC, to state legalization efforts.

The full legalization campaign revitalized efforts to cast marijuana as a dangerous drug by law enforcement agencies, which have developed new strategies that fit modern perceptions of marijuana. The old-style *Reefer Madness* fear tactics the Federal Bureau of Narcotics disseminated in the 1930s are no longer effective on a public that has enough experience with marijuana to know it does not induce psychosis, violence, or sexual deviance.

Finally, the book shows how the new industry has affected the underground one it is replacing. Deep in the hills and mountains of northern California, longtime growers are seeing huge price drops, and many believe that legalization will bring an end to an economy and a way of life that have thrived for 40 years.

As this book went to press, 14 states had legalized medical marijuana, and another 15 states had bills or initiatives in the works. Each of the 14 states had laws and restrictions tailored to its government structures and public sensibilities. For example, Oregon has a thriving medical marijuana market but does not permit dispensaries, and New Mexico is the only state that oversees large indoor growing operations. But the book mostly focuses on California, which first permitted medical marijuana and where the industry is the most developed. Other states have either adopted California's practices or rejected them as bad examples; in both cases, California has set the tone for the emerging industry, and a clear understanding of its experience will help readers understand what's happening no matter where they live.

Though not treated at length in this book, an underlying theme is the marijuana movement's relation to other social movements. The marijuana movement is unique insofar as it is morphing into a full-fledged industry that will market a product, create jobs, and generate taxes. The same cannot be said of any other modern American social rights efforts, including the labor union, suffrage, or civil rights movements. Those movements' successes resulted in abstract ideas codified in law books. In this sense, marijuana will not only be subject to the laws of man, but also to the laws of supply and demand. Some claim the end of Prohibition created a new alcohol industry, but that is not quite right. A legitimate alcohol industry had existed for hundreds of years before Prohibition. Moreover, its repeal in 1933 was not the result of a successful movement, but rather the failure of one. After decades of activism, the temperance movement had only managed to keep alcohol off the market for 13 years.

Marijuana's transformation from political movement to rapidly growing new industry is all but complete. Politicians, business associations, unions, and powerful corporations are busily preparing for a new marijuana future, one that will generate vast fortunes, new jobs, tax revenues, and campaign contributions. The marijuana movement is quickly turning into the cannabis industry—and one of the biggest political and business stories of our generation.

CHAPTER 1

Out of the Shadows

Councilman Jim Rogers had an idea to end the late-night bickering. The city council of Richmond, California, had pushed its meeting past midnight to discuss the sudden appearance of four medical marijuana dispensaries. The city's seven council members, bleary eyed and short tempered, had been discussing the issue for more than an hour. No one seemed to know where the dispensaries had come from or how to handle them. The council and city administrators were completely lost as though they were hearing for the first time that medical marijuana dispensaries had existed in California for 13 years. Constituents had been complaining to council members, who attempted to shift the blame onto department heads, who passed it around like a hot potato. The assistant police chief asked the council to recommend a course of action; the council asked for direction from the planning director, who passed it to the city attorney, who threw the whole thing back at the city council.

Then Rogers suggested his idea: why not simply ban the dispensaries? A ban would end the problem once and for all. The police would be pleased, parents would be relieved, and marijuana distributors and users wouldn't come out of the shadows to complain. The other council members agreed. They scheduled a vote on the proposed ban for the next meeting two weeks later.

Richmond sits on the northern end of the San Francisco Bay, which is ringed by some of the most progressive cities in the country. Berkeley and Oakland lie a few miles south; San Francisco and affluent Marin County are just across the bay. But Richmond's culture does not reflect its close proximity to those left-leaning cities. Although solidly Democratic, Richmond's working-class political culture tends to regard Berkeley's progressives as overeducated parlor liberals with too much time on their hands.

One example of this is the "operable" windows controversy. In 2007 Richmond's mayor, Gayle McLaughlin, proposed changing the permanently closed windows in the city's Civic Center to high-tech opening windows that were energy efficient and created a more pleasant and healthy working environment. These "operable" windows had been installed in civic buildings in Berkeley, Oakland, and San Francisco. UC Berkeley mechanical engineering professor Gail Brager made a presentation to the council citing numerous studies that verified the operable windows lowered energy costs, improved worker health, and increased productivity.[1] Nonetheless, the council majority shot down the idea. "This business about more productivity is hogwash," scoffed one councilman. "People are going to work or they aren't. Just because a window is open, all of a sudden you're going to have better performance? I don't buy it."[2]

Richmond's self-imposed isolation from its progressive neighbors may have been one reason the four dispensaries caught the city off guard. Berkeley had hammered out an effective policy a decade earlier, limiting the number of dispensaries to four and later creating a commission to oversee their operation and manage any unforeseen effects. Marin County and other Bay Area cities, including San Francisco and Oakland, had similar success governing the establishment and operation of medical marijuana dispensaries.

Richmond's next city council meeting had a long agenda, and it was past one a.m. when the council addressed the dispensary ban. By that hour, council members were usually tired from wrangling over bureaucratic details, and the public had long since gone home. But on this night, the council looked out at a sea of people who had waited hours to discuss the ban. They included medical marijuana patients, dispensary owners, attorneys, advocates, and community members. And they were spoiling to be heard.

Councilman Rogers noted the late hour and suggested the discussion be postponed until the next meeting. A loud rumbling rose up from the chamber gallery. One man's voice was clear above the others. "Go ahead and postpone it," he said. "We'll come back stronger."[3] The council decided to take up the issue.

A parade of speakers came to the lectern to argue in favor of the dispensaries and espouse the medical value of marijuana. Nearly all of them were better informed than the council members or city staff. They included representatives of Americans for Safe Access (ASA), the National Organization for the Reform of Marijuana Laws (NORML), and the newly formed Medical Cannabis Safety Council. Many of the speakers had watched the previous council meeting on video and pointed out the misconceptions, inaccuracies, and falsehoods that had been bandied about. In an orderly fashion, they accused the council of being "blatantly misleading" and "cavalier with people's medicine." They produced statistics showing that areas around dispensaries had less crime because of security patrols, surveillance cameras, and increased foot traffic. One speaker pointed out that 13 years earlier, Councilman

Rogers—then a county supervisor—had endorsed Proposition 215, the statewide measure that legalized medical marijuana. Each time the speakers concluded their remarks, the gallery erupted in raucous applause.

Of the 30 speakers who appeared, only one favored the ban on dispensaries. The hard-line attitudes the council exhibited at the previous meeting were replaced by a more open-minded approach. One of the council's most conservative members, a retired probation officer, was intrigued by the possibility of increasing the city's tax base and creating jobs. Rogers withdrew his ban proposal, and the council voted unanimously to research the advantages of allowing dispensaries to operate in Richmond. The vote produced a loud predawn cheer.

The Richmond City Council discovered that night a new and startling reality. The medical marijuana industry was not only out of the shadows, but it had become a powerful political force with savvy leadership, dedicated allies, and impressive resources.

The resources flowed from the sheer demand for the product. In California alone, the State Board of Equalization estimated the marijuana crop generated $14 billion each year, making it the state's largest cash crop—and four times bigger than the state's storied wine industry.[4] If those numbers were accurate, a fully legalized cannabis industry could contribute $1.3 billion a year in tax revenue to California's woeful coffers.[5]

Growers and dispensary owners were not the only ones making money. Ancillary businesses had also prospered. Hundreds of attorneys were counseling dispensary owners on regulatory issues, real estate law, tax strategies, business plans, and employee policies. Hundreds of doctors specialized in marijuana recommendations,[6] and insurance companies were writing policies to protect growers from crop failures. Public relations firms helped organize and design political campaigns, and lobbyists negotiated dispensary permits with local governments and advised dispensaries on community relations. While mainstream newspapers and magazines struggled to stay afloat, dozens of marijuana-based publications were thriving on advertisements for dispensaries, cultivation equipment, how-to books, and medical and legal services. Many city and county governments required dispensaries to provide comprehensive security, which had produced thousands of new low-skill jobs.

Perhaps no place demonstrates that dynamic more clearly than the commercial district in Oakland known as Oaksterdam, a play on the drug-friendly Dutch capital. Oaksterdam University, the first trade school for the medical marijuana industry, is based there. The neighborhood also has two dispensaries, a marijuana novelty and gift shop, two medical offices that specialize in marijuana recommendations, a marijuana advertising agency, law offices that specialize in marijuana issues, and a cannabis cultivation supply store. Before the marijuana industry revitalized the area, it was marked by empty storefronts, crime, and general urban decay. Now a variety of small businesses cater to students and dispensary customers, and the area has developed a hip, youthful cachet.

Faced with the industry's impressive growth, elected officials who might not have supported medical cannabis a decade ago were softening their positions. In fact, local politicians who voted to ban dispensaries not only risked losing the job growth and tax revenues that accompanied them, but also the wrath of a public that increasingly supported the medical use of marijuana and the full legalization of adult use.

Surveys have shown that a majority of every living American generation thinks medical marijuana should be legal. A 2004 poll commissioned by American Association of Retired People (AARP) discovered 72 percent of Americans 45 and older agree that adults should be allowed to legally use marijuana for medical purposes.[7] In the general population, that number was even higher. A 2010 ABC News/Washington Post poll showed 81 percent of Americans support marijuana for medical use, up from 69 percent in 1997.[8] And support for legalization of adult use was growing. A 2009 Gallup Poll showed 44 percent of Americans supported full legalization; nine years earlier, only 31 percent did so. In western states, a majority (54 percent) supported full legalization.[9]

Why the increased support after four decades of the war on drugs? One factor was demographic. Baby boomers, who grew up in an age of drug experimentation, are now running the country. Legislators and Supreme Court justices have admitted to trying marijuana, and at least three presidents have lit up. Bill Clinton famously said he tried marijuana but didn't inhale. Barack Obama said he not only inhaled in his youth, but he also did so frequently because "that was the whole point."[10] Nobody asked California governor Arnold Schwarzenegger whether or not he had smoked marijuana; anyone who has seen *Pumping Iron* (1977) knows the answer to that. Having won yet another bodybuilding title, Schwarzenegger was filmed puffing a joint at a small celebration. Medical marijuana had even been strongly endorsed by beloved national figures like PBS's travel guru Rick Steves, who somehow, with his itemized packing lists and carefully planned sightseeing schedules, seems a little more adult than most of us.

As boomers became parents, executives, managers, teachers, community leaders, and business owners, they found it difficult to argue with conviction that marijuana was the dangerous drug it was made out to be in previous decades. The philosophy student who read Jack Kerouac and listened to Charlie Parker while smoking pot is now a university regent. The high school jock who spent a year selling just enough weed so he could follow a Grateful Dead tour is now a city councilman. And the surly high school student who dyed her hair purple, strung paper-clip chains from her nose piercings, and got high while listening to Social Distortion is now a senior partner at a prestigious law firm.

As attitudes changed, so did the marijuana movement. The days of long-haired hippie advocates are over. The new cannabis advocate is clean-cut, wears a suit and tie, and often has an advanced degree or years of experience in the corporate sector. This new breed has become extraordinarily effective both in court and in shaping public opinion.

Recent court decisions in favor of the marijuana industry would have stunned the public only a decade ago. In 2008, for example, the California Department of Motor Vehicles (DMV) revoked the license of 53-year-old Rose Johnson because she had a recommendation for medical marijuana to treat a chronic back problem. Americans for Safe Access (ASA), the largest medical marijuana advocacy group in the nation, filed a suit on behalf of Johnson, who had an excellent driving record for more than 35 years. The DMV relented and reinstated Johnson's license before the case went to trial. Nonetheless, a superior court judge ordered the DMV to update its employee manual so that medical marijuana would be treated like any prescription drug. The court also required the DMV to pay $69,400 to ASA for legal fees.[11]

The courts have ordered police departments to return confiscated marijuana, provided it could be shown that the plants were cultivated for medical purposes. In 2007, a Sonoma County judge ordered the Santa Rosa Police Department to return 18 pounds of marijuana to sanctioned grower Shashon Jenkins along with about $5,000 of growing equipment. In 2008, the California Highway Patrol (CHP) stopped a driver on Highway 101 in Los Angeles and discovered 60 pounds of marijuana wrapped in one-pound bricks. When the driver's attorney showed his client was transporting the marijuana to a dispensary, the judge ordered the CHP to return it all.

The industry's political advances were even more remarkable than its court victories. Some state and local officials became unabashed champions of medical marijuana. As a result, they were able to tap prosperous donors and motivated volunteers eager to work phone banks and walk precincts for the cause. But not all local governments were so accommodating. By 2010, more than 129 California cities and counties had banned dispensaries altogether. Such bans may have been politically popular, but few believed they stopped marijuana commerce. Rather, they reinforced the old status quo, in which the marijuana trade took place on the black market. City leaders had essentially given up any chance of controlling marijuana, and the idea that law enforcement could prevent—or even significantly reduce—illegal marijuana distribution was no longer remotely viable.

Opposition to medical marijuana came from most of the expected sources: law enforcement agencies, prison guard unions, churches, and family-based organizations such as Mothers Against Drunk Driving. In cities that had allowed dispensaries with strong ordinances, police departments seemed to have accepted their presence. But in other areas, law enforcement was highly skeptical. The California Police Chiefs Association, for example, maintained a running tally of marijuana-related crimes.[12] The list included home robberies—a major problem with indoor growers—as well as property damage caused by indoor cultivation. The list also provided a record of environmental damage on private property and in state and national parks where growers dumped garbage, spilled diesel from generators, and contaminated groundwater and creeks with pesticides and herbicides. Finally, the association kept track of any murder, assault, or robbery in which marijuana was present.

Not all of these offenses were connected to medical marijuana, but a great deal of crime, environmental damage, and health and safety violations have routinely accompanied marijuana cultivation. In 2009, Los Angeles district attorney Steve Cooley tested cannabis confiscated in a dispensary raid and discovered it was laced with a pesticide used to kill Mexican fire ants.[13] In general, however, law enforcement has struggled to overcome a credibility problem created by decades of misinformation and fear tactics designed to discourage marijuana use. One California police officer admitted to me that government scare tactics have complicated meaningful debate about the issue. "I just want to discuss these issues in a real way," he said.

The opposition also included religious leaders, who argued medical marijuana advanced the interests of drug dealers. One outspoken opponent was Bishop Ron Allen, who founded the International Faith-Based Coalition. Allen said legalizing marijuana would have a devastating effect on young people and lead to more truancy, crime, and violence. He contended that marijuana is a gateway drug that leads to heavy drug use and addiction. At a 2010 rally in Sacramento, California, Allen used his own experience to back up his claims. "I grew up in Oak Park, and when a bag of pot and a pipe were handed to me, I could not resist the temptation, and I fell into a life of drugs and battling addiction," Allen said. "And now that I'm clean and sober, I see it as my calling to ensure that our youth do not slip down the dark path of drug addiction as I once did. That is why I am on a crusade to muscle all the strength of our 3,600-member International Faith-Based Coalition to ensure [legalized marijuana] never sees the light of day."[14]

Medical marijuana was not only facing outside challenges. The industry was also beginning to divide between the movement faction that championed patients' rights and the increasingly influential probusiness faction. The logical next step for the cannabis industry was full legalization, which was the stated mission of three national advocacy groups. But there were differing opinions over when and how the legalization movement should move forward.

Most of the politically active dispensaries opposed legalization because they were concerned about damage to the public image of medical marijuana. Polls showed less support for full legalization, and many activists worried that pushing for it would erode public support for medical marijuana. Dispensary owners also fretted that legalization would increase competition and lower prices in their markets, which were essentially protected by anti-marijuana laws. These concerns, however, did not stop the aggressive pursuit of full legalization. One initiative, Control and Tax 2010, qualified for California's November 2010 ballot. If successful, it would be a game changer for California and the rest of the country.

By 2010, the public debate about marijuana had been transformed. The main theme was no longer how to eliminate the plucky weed by beefing up law enforcement. Instead, discussions focused on how to distribute marijuana safely. In fact, the culture had become so marijuana-friendly, the U.S. government's 40-year campaign to demonize weed became a distant memory.

CHAPTER 2

Damnation

For anyone old enough to recall flashes of paranoia while smoking a joint at home, marijuana's new social prominence is striking. But a younger generation has grown up in communities where police officers write tickets for possession of a joint or two. For these young people, marijuana has never been a scary substance that could somehow ruin their lives. Even if they live in a state where medical marijuana is illegal, they know that in other states, marijuana can be purchased in storefronts—or even delivered to one's home, like a pizza.

This cannabis-tolerant generation is not, in fact, America's first. In the nineteenth century, cannabis was a common commodity sold in various forms as an over-the-counter remedy. Far from being considered evil, it was regarded as an affordable palliative that medical associations had approved for a host of ailments. Its stature changed only in the twentieth century, when the U.S. government recast marijuana as a dangerous narcotic. That campaign was so successful that it's difficult today to appreciate how immense the government's task was.

Marijuana's initial acceptance as a medicine began with the

inquiries of an ambitious young Irish doctor on the other side of the world. William Brooke O'Shaughnessy was born in Limerick, Ireland, to a conservative Catholic family. He was a bright student and was eventually accepted to the University of Edinburgh Medical School. Shortly after graduating in 1830, the 24-year-old O'Shaughnessy went to work in Bengal, India, as an assistant surgeon and a professor of chemistry at a medical college in Calcutta.[1] Almost immediately he began an intensive study of oriental texts on hashish. O'Shaughnessy learned what he could from native doctors and scholars in Tehran, Kabul, and Kandahar, and he began his own experiments on stray dogs, which were plentiful in India. Once he saw hashish had no lasting ill effects on the dogs, he began experiments with humans.

O'Shaughnessy administered hashish oil to patients suffering from illnesses such as rheumatism, tetanus, cholera, and epilepsy. Hashish didn't cure any of these maladies, but it proved valuable as an effective analgesic and sedative. Six years after arriving in India, O'Shaughnessy presented the first modern medical paper on marijuana and hashish to the Medical and Physical Society of Bengal. In the paper, O'Shaughnessy concluded that hashish was "an anti-convulsive remedy of the greatest value." He also detailed traditional recipes for making Majoon, a hemp confection made with sugar, butter, flour, milk, and a paste called *sidhee* or bang, which is formed by the large leaves and stalks of the cannabis plant. According to O'Shaughnessy's research, the sweet thin cake was used recreationally and to increase the libido. "It is most fascinating in its effects, producing ecstatic happiness, a persuasion of high rank, a sensation of flying—voracious appetite, and intense aphrodisiac desire," O'Shaughnessy wrote.[2]

During a visit to England in 1842, O'Shaughnessy gave some

hashish to a London pharmacist named Peter Squire, who made the first reported extract of hashish in alcohol. He patented it as Squire's Extract and put it on the market as an analgesic pain reliever. Other pharmacists began to market cannabis extracts. One was James Smith of Edinburgh, whose Tilden's Extract was sold in America. Squire's Extract and other tinctures soon became widely used because they were a sensible alternative to opium, the only other painkiller on the market. Opium was expensive, highly addictive, and had unpleasant side effects such as constipation, itching, loss of appetite, and lowering of heart and respiratory rates.[3] The United States Pharmacopoeia described it as an appropriate application for the treatment of neuralgia, tetanus, typhus, cholera, rabies, dysentery, alcoholism and opiate addiction, anthrax, leprosy, incontinence, snake bite, gout, virtually any disease that induced convulsions, tonsillitis, insanity, menorrhagia (excessive menstrual bleeding), and uterine hemorrhaging.

The new drug received a boost when word went out that Queen Victoria's physician, Sir John Russell Reynolds, prescribed a cannabis-based extract to his number one patient for menstrual cramps. A great deal of research on cannabis extracts, including their psychological effects, began to appear in the United States. By 1887, Hobart Amory Hare described the drug's ability to reduce the anxiety of those suffering from terminal illnesses. He also discussed its effect on the perceived passage of time.

> During the time that this remarkable drug is relieving pain a very curious physical condition manifests itself: namely, that the diminution of the pain seems to be due to its fading away in the distance, so the pain becomes less and less, just as the pain in a delicate ear would grow less and less as a beaten drum was carried farther and farther out of the range of hearing. This

condition is probably associated with the other well-known symptom produced by the drug: namely, the prolongation of time.[4]

The research popularized the new drug, and affordable cannabis extracts were readily available as over-the-counter remedies. In Britain, middle-class women preferred cannabis to alcohol, which they considered masculine and common.

American pharmaceutical companies were busily marketing cannabis tinctures as patent cures. E.R. Squib & Sons offered Chlorodyne and Corn Collodium; Parke Davis sold Utroval and Casadein. Eli Lilly produced Dr. Brown's Sedative Tablets, Neurosine, and the one-day Cough Cure, which directly competed with a product called Dreser made by the German pharmaceutical company Bayer. Snuff made from a combination of tobacco and cannabis was used as an asthma cure. Grimault and Sons marketed "Indian Cigarettes," which were essentially prerolled joints, as a treatment for asthma and coughs that had the additional benefit of inducing sleep in insomniacs.

Despite the wide selection of cannabis-based medicines, problems arose. Cannabis-processing inconsistencies made it nearly impossible for manufacturers to manage dosages. Often medicines made by the same company varied in strength, which made some doctors wary of prescribing them. Unlike opiates, which are water soluble, cannabis medicines could not be injected. That meant it could take hours for extracts to take effect. Finally, cannabis preparations would separate if left standing. Residue would form at the bottom of the bottle, and if not properly agitated before consumption, it could cause overdose. Some medical journals referred to the overdosing as "cannabis poisoning," even though cannabis is nontoxic. The term described a strong hallucinogenic reaction after patients ingested the residue at the bottom of medicine bottles.

These problems put cannabis on shaky ground among physicians, but what finally made it medically obsolete was the advent of synthetic drugs. The beginning of the end for cannabis extracts occurred in 1853, when a French chemist Charles Frederick Gerhardt produced acetylsalicylic acid. Just before the turn of the century, Bayer was marketing a refined version of Gerhardt's concoction as aspirin. For a few years afterward, cannabis tinctures were still used to ease muscle cramps and insomnia, but that was soon to end. The British Medical Association launched a campaign against the mysterious ingredients of patent medicines and took aim at eliminating opiates, cocaine, and cannabis from a host of nonprescription elixirs and tonics. Although synthetics were potentially more harmful than nontoxic cannabis, the medical community preferred them because their effects were more predictable.[5]

From Medication to Recreation

The medical uses of cannabis faded quickly, but during the first three decades of the twentieth century, the highly adaptable plant established itself as a recreational drug in nearly every major U.S. city.

The migration of nonmedical cannabis to the United States isn't officially documented, but the general consensus is the first leg of the trip was from Africa to South America. One school of thought is that African slaves carried cannabis seeds sewn inside of talismanic dolls when they were brought to work on Brazilian sugar plantations in the first half of the sixteenth century. Another theory is that Portuguese sailors brought them directly to the New World from Portuguese settlements in India. In any case, cannabis cultivation began on Brazilian sugar plantations mostly in the northeast, and African slaves introduced cannabis smoking to the native Indian population.

Cannabis smoking was slow to take hold among Indians, who already had a full menu of psychotropic options, including peyote and mescaline as well as stimulants like coca. But cannabis slowly migrated northward to Mexico, where it was first officially noted in 1880. By the turn of the century, cannabis was growing freely throughout the country, and peasants were cultivating it to smoke in pipes or to add it to infusions with sugar cane sap, milk, and chilies. It was in Mexico that cannabis picked up a new name, "marijuana," assumed to be a combination of the Spanish pronunciation of "Mary" and "Jane," which were slang terms for a prostitute or a brothel. By 1900, *marijuana* was part of Mexico's national lexicon, and the drug itself was poised to complete the final leg of its journey to the United States by route of Texas.

With the start of the Mexican Revolution in 1910, hundreds of thousands of Mexicans migrants crossed the Rio Grande. They brought the practice of smoking cannabis, which was legal in the United States, along with them. The high demand for marijuana in Texas towns like Corpus Christi, San Antonio, and Austin fostered new companies that specialized in importing marijuana from Mexico. Revolutionary general Pancho Villa had been known to raid towns and ranches just across the U.S. border to keep his troops supplied with marijuana. Villa's troops were culled from peasants, nearly all of whom smoked marijuana as a form of relaxation and to gear up for battle. The folk song "La Cucaracha" was a jaunty, self-deprecating ditty about cockroaches, which Villa's troops nicknamed themselves.

The cockroach, the cockroach,
Now it cannot walk,
Because it doesn't have, because it lacks
Marijuana to smoke.

Villa's incursions and the migration of Mexican immigrants into the American southwest created mistrust and racial hostility. Landowners began to hire Mexican laborers for low wages, which outraged labor unions. White Americans deemed them un-American because of their language and their penchant for smoking marijuana. Although Texas law enforcement officials lacked factual evidence, they began claiming that marijuana caused crime and violence. Describing Mexicans as "marijuana fiends," El Paso citizens approved the first local law forbidding the possession and use of marijuana. Ironically, California became the first state to outlaw marijuana in 1913, and southern state legislators lobbied Washington to take action against the "loco weed" on a federal level.

Marijuana was also making inroads in New Orleans, whose thriving port attracted sailors from the Caribbean and West Indies. Many were marijuana runners, and by 1915, marijuana was being used by dockworkers, prostitutes, field hands, and jazz musicians. In Storyville, the red-light district where jazz was born, drugs were common. New Orleans officials closed Storyville in 1917 in an effort to clean up the city. The closure sparked an exodus of blacks, including jazz musicians, who found work in Chicago, Kansas City, and elsewhere. By 1930, marijuana had spread to Denver, Detroit, San Francisco, Baltimore, Cleveland, St. Louis, and other major cities.

The spread of marijuana coincided with an international temperance movement. An international effort to curb opium use began with the first meeting of the Shanghai Opium Commission in 1909 and culminated with the International Opium Convention in the Hague in 1912. By the time the commission met in 1925, there was pressure to add cannabis to the list of dangerous drugs. In the United States, meanwhile, the temperance movement enabled the passage of the Volstead Act of 1919, which prohibited the consumption of alcohol until its repeal in 1933.

Prohibition was the result of a large, complex social movement. But shortly after alcohol was criminalized, one man launched a national anti-marijuana campaign so effective that its effects linger to this day.

The Anslinger Campaign

Whatever else Prohibition accomplished, it defined the career of Harry J. Anslinger. A trustworthy and skillful diplomat, Anslinger earned his reputation by coordinating an international effort to bust European rumrunners smuggling alcohol into the United States. In 1929, he was promoted to assistant commissioner of the Prohibition Unit; the following year, he became the first head of the newly created Federal Bureau of Narcotics (FBN). His commanding presence, powerful connections, and facility with the press made him a formidable bureaucrat.[6]

Anslinger had a cannabis fixation almost from the time he became head of the FBN. Over the next 32 years, he used his skills to demonize the drug through a fear-based campaign untethered by facts or scientific study. Anslinger found a willing partner in William Randolph Hearst, whose newspaper empire became an important tool for anti-marijuana propaganda. It was in Hearst's newspapers that the term marijuana (then spelled "marihuana") became popular in the United States.

Marijuana had long been known as hemp among those who didn't smoke it, but Anslinger was so keen to give marijuana a bad name that he even distorted its etymology. According to Anslinger, the ancient Aztecs called cannabis "malihua" or "mallihuan," which was made up of the elements "mallin," which means prisoner, "hua," which loosely means property, and the verb "ana," or to capture or grab. Anslinger claimed that marijuana meant "captured prisoner" or "addict."

Etymological gymnastics were only part of Anslinger's campaign. In 1935, he saw to it that marijuana was included in the FBN's annual reports, which had previously focused on opiates and cocaine. Anslinger also began to circulate stories about evil deeds committed by people, mostly Mexican immigrants and blacks, while under the influence of cannabis. Anslinger played up the idea that marijuana led to promiscuity and homosexuality. Hearst's Universal News Service was only too eager to help spread the word. One story, which was richer in melodrama than facts, appeared in 1936 under the headline "Murders Due to 'Killer Drug' Marihuana Sweeping the United States." The story read, "Shocking crimes of violence are increasing. Murders, slaughterings, cruel mutilations, maimings, done in cold blood, as if some hideous monster was amok in the land . . . much of the violence [is attributed to] what experts call marihuana . . . a roadside weed in almost every State in the Union . . . Those addicted . . . lose all restraints, all inhibitions. They become bestial demoniacs, filled with a mad lust to kill. . . ."[7]

Anslinger's favorite story was of a 21-year-old Florida resident named Victor Licata. One October morning in 1933, Licata used an axe to kill his parents, two brothers, and a sister while they slept in their beds. Anslinger claimed Licata told police he committed the crimes while in a "marihuana dream." Anslinger also claimed Licata had been smoking cannabis regularly for six months prior to the murders. In fact, there was a history of mental illness among Licata's parents and immediate family members, some of whom had been committed to asylums. Police had attempted to commit Licata to an asylum almost a year before the killings, but his parents intervened and agreed to take care of him themselves. After the killings, Licata was diagnosed with "dementia praecox with homicidal tendencies." There was no mention of marijuana anywhere in Licata's medical records.[8] But Anslinger was not one to let the facts get in the way of a good story.

Anslinger was said to have a repertoire of 200 such tales, which he circulated through newspapers, magazines, and radio broadcasts. In one article, which appeared in the *American Magazine*, Anslinger wrote:

The sprawled body of a young girl lay crushed on the sidewalk the other day after a plunge from the fifth story of a Chicago apartment house. Everyone called it suicide, but actually it was murder. The killer was a narcotic known in America as marihuana, and to history as hashish. It is a narcotic used in the form of cigarettes, comparatively new to the United States and as dangerous as a coiled rattlesnake.[9]

Another favorite recounted more pot-fueled violence:

In Los Angeles, a youth was walking along a downtown street after inhaling a marihuana cigarette. For many addicts, merely a portion of a "reefer" is enough to induce intoxication. Suddenly, for no reason, he decided that someone had threatened to kill him and that his life at that very moment was in danger. Wildly he looked about him. The only person in sight was an aged bootblack. Drug-crazed nerve centers conjured the innocent old shoe-shiner into a destroying monster. Mad with fright, the addict hurried to his room and got a gun. He killed the old man, and then, later babbled his grief over what had been wanton, uncontrolled murder. "I thought someone was after me," he said. "That's the only reason I did it. I had never seen the old fellow before. Something just told me to kill him!" That's marihuana![10]

Anslinger's dramatic tales soon found their way into the movies. In 1935, the film *Marihuana* was released with the tagline "Weird orgies! Wild parties! Unleashed passions!" The most famous anti-marijuana film was released in 1936 as *Tell Your Children*, though it would become widely known as *Reefer Madness*. The plot follows high school students Mae and Jack, who introduce marijuana to their schoolmates. The drug quickly turns each of their lives to shambles. One student is even committed to an insane asylum for life.

Much of Anslinger's campaign was tinged with racism. In the mid-1930s, he began writing articles about marijuana-induced rapes and murders in which the victims were usually white and the suspects almost always black or Hispanic.[11] In 1934, Anslinger went too far when he referred to a black man in one of his anti-marijuana pamphlets as a "ginger-colored nigger." Black community leaders in Pennsylvania, where the pamphlet was distributed, were outraged, and the ensuing uproar would have cost Anslinger his job in the Roosevelt administration if he hadn't had the strong support of newspaper editors, conservative congressmen, and the pharmaceutical companies.

Anslinger also did what he could to discourage scientific study of marijuana. The lack of unbiased scientific study was critical to Anslinger's propaganda goals because it allowed him to make wild claims about marijuana's negative effects on society and its association with crime particularly among Mexicans and blacks. The lack of study also preempted experts from challenging his unproven claims.

Within a few years, Anslinger's anti-marijuana campaign began to show results. Thirty-eight states added marijuana to their most dangerous drugs list under the Uniform State Narcotics Acts. Those that didn't put marijuana on the list took steps to control its sale and possession.

In 1937, Anslinger set his sights on a federal bill. He stepped up his speaking engagements, which featured his horror stories. Meanwhile, Herman Oliphant, the Treasury Department's chief counsel, began to draft the bill that would levy a punitive transfer tax on marijuana, as the federal government had done on automatic machine guns. The tax was the only constitutional option open to Anslinger for controlling marijuana on a federal level. The bill would ultimately be known as the Marihuana Tax Act of 1937.

The preliminary hearings were little more than a sequel to Anslinger's nationwide smear campaign. No bona fide statistics or scientific facts were presented, and the expert testimony offered little more than warmed-over Anslinger stories. At one point, Anslinger asked Dr. Carl Voegtlin, the chief of pharmacology at the National Institutes of Health, if smoking marijuana led to insanity. Voegtlin responded, "I think it is an established fact that prolonged use leads to insanity in certain cases."

Major opposition to the bill came from Dr. William C. Woodward of the American Medical Association (AMA), who objected to the act because FBN agents had arrested or threatened thousands of doctors on prescription charges under the 1914 Harrison Narcotics Tax Act, which limited physicians' authority to prescribe opiates and their derivatives. Woodward, who was also an attorney, pointed out that the entire hearing process was one-sided and rushed, and that the testimony was vague and lacking in scientific evidence. However, Woodward's objections did nothing to slow the bill's passage through the House and the Senate. President Roosevelt signed the new tax in August, and the first federal law controlling marijuana went into effect in October.

Anslinger had achieved many of his goals in a relatively short time. The FBN's budget soared, and the American people now believed that marijuana was a menace plaguing the country. Ironically, Anslinger's success created new problems for his agency. The public now expected to see arrests, deportations, and eradication programs. But the marijuana problem described by Anslinger was a fiction, and those who did use the drug regularly were difficult to identify and prosecute, especially as the marijuana hysteria heated up. With few resources at the local level, Angslinger was unable to enforce the new act in a meaningful way, but his campaign created a deeply rooted fear of marijuana in the American psyche.

As the nation would soon learn, marijuana was nothing if not resilient; it could withstand smear campaigns as well as substandard soil. Well before Anslinger's retirement in 1961, marijuana had already begun its comeback.

Beats and Hippies

As much as any place, San Francisco was the foundry in which Proposition 215 was cast. Ever since the gold rush, the city had attracted seekers and rebels. In the 1950s, that group included a small clique of writers and free spirits who were challenging American social and literary orthodoxies. Later known as the Beats, they included poet Allen Ginsberg, novelist Jack Kerouac, and Neal Cassady, a fast-talking car thief and speed freak. The Beats identified more with the counterculture world of jazz musicians and European literary movements than with Eisenhower-era conformity. They studied Buddhism, traveled restlessly, and experimented with new forms of writing that relied heavily on spontaneous thoughts. In search of intense experiences, they also sampled a wide variety of drugs, including heroin, cocaine, peyote, and marijuana.

In the early 1950s, San Francisco was still a relatively inexpensive city, and the Beats found a home in North Beach, an Italian neighborhood where working-class immigrants owned most of the restaurants, cafés, and delicatessens. Many had come from impoverished sections of Italy where there was little access to radios, movie theaters, or even a local playhouse. For entertainment, they relied on circuses and small theater groups that traveled through the Italian countryside. The Italians welcomed these performers warmly, and they were willing to overlook their sometimes overdramatic, boorish, and drunken behavior. When the Beats began to arrive in North Beach, the locals enjoyed their liveliness and hardly noticed their loud verse, histrionics, and drunken antics.

By 1952, Neal Cassady had married, taken a job with the railroad, and made a home in San Francisco. But he believed smoking marijuana was a joyful experience that should be shared with as many people as possible. His railroad job regularly took him into Mexico, and he began to smuggle large quantities of marijuana back to the United States in boxcars. In San Francisco, Cassady

usually gave the weed away rather than selling it, and he is generally thought to be the person who started large-scale marijuana
use in California.

In October 1955, the Beats presaged a generation of social
upheaval when Allen Ginsberg read his poem "Howl" to a group
of writers that included Kerouac, Gary Snyder, Phillip Whalen,
and Michael McClure at the Six Gallery. "Howl" referred explic-
itly to drug use and gay sex, including one controversial line about
those "who let themselves be fucked in the ass by saintly motor-
cyclists, and screamed with joy." Obscenity charges were brought
against Lawrence Ferlinghetti, the owner of City Lights bookstore
in North Beach and the poem's publisher. After 90 literary experts
testified on the poem's behalf, Judge Clayton Horn decided it had
some literary value. The widely publicized case raised the Beats'
profile and drew thousands of restless souls to North Beach, where
they attended poetry readings, listened to jazz, and experimented
with marijuana.

After the success of Kerouac's novel *On the Road*, that migration continued. Cassady, whom Kerouac used as a model for the
character of Dean Moriarty, continued to provide marijuana to
the newcomers. But his luck ran out in early 1958, when he was
arrested in a drug sting and received a sentence of two years to life.
After serving two and half years in San Quentin, he was released.[12]

The authorities may have stopped Cassady from supplying
marijuana, but its popularity continued to grow, and it became
the celebrated mainstay of a new social movement originating in
San Francisco's Haight-Ashbury neighborhood. This counterculture emphasized radical politics, psychedelic experience, sexual
freedom, and environmental awareness. Like the Beats, San Francisco's hippies liked to get high, but they were less troubled by

alienation and despair. LSD, which was legal until 1966, became a popular Haight-Ashbury drug, and marijuana use was especially common.

As the Bay Area counterculture flourished, it played a central role in the nation's antiwar, civil rights, and environmental movements. It had also put marijuana on the national stage, and the robust little weed became a symbol of rebellion and personal freedom. According to the U.S. Department of Health and Human Services, less than a half-million Americans had tried marijuana by 1965. Four years later, that number had soared to just under 15 million.[13]

The Haight scene collapsed in the late 1960s, and some of its residents joined the back-to-the-land movement. Settling the counties north of San Francisco that would eventually become known as the Emerald Triangle, many back-to-the-landers began cultivating marijuana in earnest. But the activism that would lead directly to Proposition 215 was taking place in another San Francisco neighborhood: the Castro.

CHAPTER 3

Redemption

While the Beats and hippies certainly popularized marijuana use, the medical marijuana movement's direct precursor was San Francisco's gay rights movement of the 1970s. Centered in the city's Castro district, the movement was headed by Harvey Milk and organized to defeat ballot measures directed at gay teachers and renters. Milk would go on to become the first openly gay man on the San Francisco Board of Supervisors, and his legacy influenced a generation of younger activists.

One of them was Dennis Peron, a close friend and a political student of Milk's. A Vietnam veteran and confirmed hippie, Peron settled in the Castro in 1972 and began selling the pot he had smuggled back from Vietnam. He moved friends into a large two-bedroom flat, which became known as the Big Top Commune. Because Peron was also selling significant quantities of marijuana from the flat, it soon had another nickname: The Supermarket.

Peron was eventually arrested and sentenced to a work furlough program. During this time, he opened The Island, a restaurant which seated 250 people and became a popular location for political meetings and benefits. Another reason for its popularity was the fact that

Peron was selling marijuana from an upstairs apartment, an enterprise that at one time employed 20 people. In June 1977, the apartment was raided, and a police officer shot Peron in the upper leg, where the bullet remains lodged. One story goes that Peron thought the raid was a robbery, and he intended to throw a bottle at the suspected marauders. Another is that Peron was angry at yet another bust and was about to throw a bottle at the cops out of frustration.

Police confiscated 200 pounds of marijuana, and Peron was facing serious prison time. But the case against him began to fall apart when the officer who had shot Peron approached him in the courthouse hallway, called him a "motherfucking faggot," and said he wished he had killed him so there would be one less faggot in San Francisco. The officer's testimony was thrown out, and the district attorney offered Peron a sentence of six months in jail, which he accepted. Peron used the notoriety of the raid to collect 16,000 signatures for a city ballot measure to legalize marijuana. Measure W failed, but Peron had launched his first political action and learned he was effective at it.

While Peron was carrying on his guerrilla activism, Bay Area politicians were paralleling his efforts with legislation. The area's progressives had a reputation for embracing new ideas. The city of Berkeley, for example, pioneered wheelchair curb cuts, curbside recycling, urban wildlands preservation, and the first government-sponsored solar panel–financing program. And Bay Area progressives were among the first to call for the legalization of marijuana. In the 1970s, San Francisco attorney Leo Paoli inspired a wave of pro-marijuana legislation from San Francisco politicians. Paoli authored the California Marijuana Initiative and was able to collect enough signatures to put the first-ever marijuana legalization initiative on the California ballot in 1972. The initiative received only 34 percent of the vote and lost every county in the state but one, San Francisco.[1]

But savvy city politicians realized they had local support for marijuana legislation. In 1974, state senator George Moscone formed a select committee and charged it with examining marijuana laws. The committee recommended decriminalization, and Moscone introduced Senate Bill 95, whose passage made California the fifth state to decriminalize the possession of small amounts of marijuana.

Meanwhile the medical marijuana movement had begun to take shape. The idea of legalizing marijuana for medical purposes gained prominence in 1975 when Robert Randall, who suffered from glaucoma, was arrested for cultivating marijuana for his personal use. Randall won his Washington, DC, superior court case in 1976 by using the "medical necessity defense."[2] A subsequent lawsuit forced the Department of Public Health to create the Compassionate Investigational New Drug program, which provided Randall and six other patients with prerolled marijuana that had been grown by the University of Mississippi. By becoming the first person granted the legal right to use marijuana for medical purposes, Randall shifted the focus of the marijuana reform movement away from the legalization of adult use and toward the legalization of medical use.

San Francisco politicians quickly developed the first legislation to legalize marijuana for medical use. Moscone, who had become mayor in 1976, joined Republican state senator Milton Marks and supervisor Harvey Milk in 1977 to support the San Francisco Marijuana Initiative known as Measure W. The measure won, by a wide margin, but was trumped by state law and therefore unenforceable.

In 1978, two incidents rocked the San Francisco political community. The first was the Jonestown Massacre, in which 918 persons, many of them impoverished people of color from San Francisco, died in a remote jungle in northwestern Guyana. Jim Jones, leader of the Peoples Temple, ordered several of his followers to kill Congressman Leo Ryan and members of his delegation, who were visiting the outpost on a fact-finding mission. Jones then commanded his followers to commit mass suicide by drinking cyanide-laced Kool-Aid. In an unrelated incident nine days later, former supervisor Dan White shot and killed Moscone and Milk at city hall.

A stunned city took a step back. That year, Democrat Dianne Feinstein, a law-and-order moderate, succeeded Moscone as mayor. Over the next decade, she focused on developing the downtown area and keeping the city quiet. The rest of the country was also ready for more conservative politics and elected Ronald Reagan president in 1980. He launched one of the most aggressive anti-drug campaigns the country had seen in decades, and marijuana was one of the primary targets.

The marijuana movement went into hiatus but regained momentum as a result of a crisis. In the 1980s, the AIDS epidemic swept through the country's gay communities, and San Francisco was hit particularly hard. Many AIDS victims were using marijuana to help them cope with various symptoms. The drug was particularly helpful with AIDS Wasting Syndrome, which was caused by a lack of appetite.

When Peron's lover, Jonathan West, contracted AIDS in the late 1980s, he used marijuana to treat his symptoms. But Peron remained a police target, and during a 1991 raid on their home, Peron watched as police roughed up West during a search for marijuana. In jail, Peron decided he would do whatever it took to change marijuana laws. Shortly after West died, Peron led a signature-gathering campaign that resulted in San Francisco's Proposition P, which recommended the state of California put cannabis on the list of state-approved medicines. The proposition had no teeth legally, but it had the support of the Board of Supervisors and won a stunning 79 percent of the vote. Similar local initiatives calling for the legalization of medical marijuana followed in Santa Cruz and other cities around the state.

Peron's Proposition P had reignited the medical momentum, and it was even stronger than before. For one thing, support on the San Francisco Board of Supervisors increased. Supervisor Terence Hallinan, who came from a long line of pugnacious activists, was a strong champion of medical marijuana. His grandfather was the leader of the Great Front Strike in 1899, and his father, Vincent Hallinan, was a firebrand attorney who once sued the Roman Catholic Church for fraud, demanding it prove the existence of heaven and hell.[3] He was perhaps best known for representing controversial union leader Harry Bridges. Terence Hallinan was as combative as his father and even more committed to progressive politics. In 1991, he called for the San Francisco Police Department and district attorney's office to make the possession or cultivation of marijuana their lowest priority for arrests or prosecution. The resolution also urged law enforcement to consider letters from a physician stating marijuana was being used for medical purposes. The resolution was approved by a unanimous vote of the Board of Supervisors and signed by Mayor Frank Jordan, a former police chief.

Statewide support for medical marijuana was also growing, but when Milton Marks and Democratic assemblyman John Vasconcellos succeeded in getting the legislature to approve their bill to legalize marijuana, Republican governor Pete Wilson vetoed it without much ceremony.

The Cannabis Buyers' Club

In 1994, a frustrated Peron took a leap of faith and opened California's first marijuana dispensary, the Cannabis Buyers' Club, at 1444 Market Street. He had the blessing of the city's Board of Supervisors, and Supervisor Tom Ammiano attended the opening celebration and participated in the ribbon cutting. The club set the standard for medicinal marijuana distribution that continues to this day. "I rented a large building, decorated it, and opened for business," Peron wrote in *Brownie Mary's Marijuana Cookbook*. "The club started out about marijuana, but has ended up being about a lot more. It turned into a place where lonely, sick people can help each other and not be alone."[4]

The "Five-Story Felony," as Peron liked to call it, offered social activities to help very ill patients fight the common symptom of social withdrawal. On certain days, massages, haircuts, and food were available for free along with a regular supply of cannabis-based edibles and cooking oils. There was an entertainment area, a softball team, and plenty of opportunity to become involved with political organizations. Some of the most respected growers in the state taught cannabis cultivation courses there.

But by opening the club, Peron was defying the law as much as he was helping AIDS patients. Peron's chutzpah began to inspire other activists. One was Jeff Jones, a lanky 20-year-old from the high plains of South Dakota. Like many in the medical marijuana movement, Jones was motivated by the death of a loved one—his father, who died of cancer when Jones was 14. The death was particularly emotional, Jones said, because his father's last days were spent in a home hospice. That same year, federal judge Francis Young ruled that under medical supervision, marijuana had value for certain illnesses. He ordered its removal from the Schedule I list of narcotics (which includes dangerous drugs without medical value), though ultimately, this did not happen. In his ruling, Judge Young famously described marijuana as "one of the safest therapeutically active substances known to man."[5]

The ruling was troubling to Jones. Even though his father had never wanted to use marijuana as a treatment, Jones was outraged that the government continued to deny access to a medicine that could bring comfort to the dying despite Young's ruling. Jones had never been politically active, but the issue triggered something in him. In 1994, Jones dropped out of college, went home to gather some belongings, and announced, to the dismay of his family, that he was heading west to the San Francisco Bay Area where he would become a medical marijuana activist. "I came to California with a footlocker and a backpack," Jones said. "I didn't have a mortgage, a marriage, or a kid—those things that tie you down in our social infrastructure. The things that make you . . . behave. I was going to try and do something different."[6]

Within a week of his arrival, Jones made the trip to Peron's Cannabis Buyers' Club. Soon he crossed the bay and opened the Oakland Cannabis Buyers' Club (the name was later changed to Oakland Cannabis Buyers' Cooperative) on the fifth floor of 1755 Broadway, just around the corner from city hall. Like Peron, he had the blessing of the city council, but was not protected by city, state, or federal law. Looking back, Jones said it was best if marijuana activists were not particularly attached to anything: family, career, wealth, or even freedom.

Jones started by taking home delivery orders for medical marijuana. A lack of resources precluded a company vehicle, so when orders came in, Jones delivered them on his maroon Giant bicycle (which he still owns) covered with political bumper stickers. Within a year, the club purchased a delivery vehicle, which greatly increased its delivery area. Jones was also one of the first activists to bring a professional fashion sense to the industry. At demonstrations, in city council meetings, and during court appearances, Jones was always clad in suit and tie. With his closely cropped hair and serious disposition, he looked more like a corporate attorney than a medical marijuana activist.

While Peron's club was selling medical marijuana at a good clip, he began working with his colleagues in the medical marijuana movement to author a state ballot initiative. Along with registered nurse Anna Boyce, Valerie Corral, Dale Gieringer, William Pranzer, Scott Imler, and psychiatrist Tod H. Mikuriya, Peron wrote Proposition 215. The authors then began circulating petitions to gather the 400,000 signatures required to qualify the initiative for the November 1996 state ballot. As the deadline approached, it became clear the volunteer signature-gathering effort would fail. But a group of philanthropists, including George Soros and George Zimmer, funded a company that specialized in circulating petitions, and it succeeded in gathering the necessary signatures.

By the time Proposition 215 was on the ballot, AIDS had ravaged the San Francisco gay community for more than 10 years. The epidemic had evoked sympathy throughout the state, and because it was widely accepted that marijuana helped offset the wasting effects of AIDS, that sympathy translated into support for Proposition 215. Studies also showed that marijuana countered the effects of chemotherapy, which reinforced its medical status in the public mind.

Proposition 215 received widespread endorsements from elected officials throughout the state. But conservative lawmakers, California attorney general Dan Lungren, and a coalition of law enforcement agencies, vigorously opposed it. Washington, DC, was also watching. President Bill Clinton was so alarmed that 215 might pass that he encouraged former presidents George Bush and Jimmy Carter to join him in opposing the proposition. The three issued a letter denouncing California's proposition as well as a related one in Arizona that would allow doctors to write marijuana prescriptions. "Given the resurgent drug use by our youth, these measures pose enormous threats to the public health of Arizonians, Californians, and all Americans," the letter reads. Despite the opposition, more than 55 percent of California voters approved the first medical marijuana law in the United States. Arizonans also approved their ballot measure, which allowed doctors to prescribe marijuana, but did not address distribution.

By that time, Hallinan had been elected San Francisco district attorney, the only one in the state to endorse Proposition 215. One of his political opponents, conservative state senator Quentin Kopp, summed up Hallinan's role as outsider. "There are 58 counties in California, 57 of which have tough district attorneys. Then there is Terence. He is definitely one of a kind."

Hallinan remained a champion of medical marijuana until he lost a bid for a third term in 2003. The night Hallinan lost, the *San Francisco Chronicle* published a story that described a small group of people smoking pot outside Hallinan's campaign office. "Terence Hallinan is the only prosecutor in the nation who had a handful of supporters smoking 'medical' marijuana outside his campaign office," the article reads. "Their mere presence on election night highlighted the vast difference between Hallinan and the criminal justice system."[7]

The Aftermath

Proposition 215 became law, but not without problems. It was riddled with vagueness, gaps, and oversights. Police agencies weren't sure what was legal, and local governments were clueless on regulating the cultivation, possession, and distribution of medical marijuana. Making things worse, federal and state law enforcement agencies were planning a campaign to squash the fledgling law and discourage other states from following California's lead.

New challenges soon presented themselves. California attorney general Dan Lungren was determined to hamper the new law's implementation in any way possible. President Bill Clinton's drug czar, Barry McCaffrey, supported Lungren and offered him all of the federal support he could use to prevent the medical marijuana movement from taking hold. Clinton announced plans to prosecute any physicians that prescribed medical marijuana. The Clinton Administration wanted to make sure that California and Arizona would be the last two states to legalize medical marijuana, despite its popular support.

Meanwhile, liberal cities such as Oakland, San Francisco, and San Jose were struggling to regulate dispensaries. Because many anti-marijuana laws were still on the books, that task was especially daunting. One gap in particular was causing problems. Proposition 215 had no provisions for cultivation, transportation, and possession. Patients and caregivers were not protected from arrest for possession, though they were provided with an immunity defense should they be charged. The law also had no provision allowing caregivers remuneration for providing cannabis to patients. Because of these gaps and others, cities had troubles regulating distribution and personal cultivation.

The oversight was illustrated when the Butte County Sheriff's Department raided the Chico home of Bryan James Epis in 1997. Sheriff's deputies arrested Epis for a grow operation in his basement. Deputies confiscated 458 plants, most of which were seedlings. Epis, who suffered from chronic pain related to a traffic accident, had a doctor's recommendation and was growing medical marijuana for a small medical marijuana cooperative he had organized called the Chico Medical Marijuana Caregivers. Epis was the first medical marijuana patient to be arrested after the passage of Proposition 215. His arrest became national news, and he became a hero in the medical marijuana movement.

But Epis would soon become a martyr as well. The Butte County sheriff turned the case over to the Drug Enforcement Administration (DEA), which was keen to squash any marijuana activities related to Proposition 215, and Epis was tried under the federal Controlled Substances Act. His defense was prohibited from mentioning the term medical marijuana, and Epis received a 10-year sentence.

The Epis case made it clear the new law needed clarification. State senator John Vasconcellos and assemblyman Mark Leno introduced Senate Bill 420 to give clear guidelines to local government, state law enforcement agencies, and patients. SB 420 set default limits of 6 mature plants and 12 immature plants, and eight ounces of dried, processed pot, but it also allowed counties and cities to raise those limits if they chose to. Oakland, for example, raised the default limit to 72 plants and three pounds of dried, processed marijuana. SB 420 also allowed for the transportation of medical cannabis, intent to distribute, processing, sale, and maintaining a place where cannabis is used or produced; allowed caregivers to be reimbursed for growing and providing medical marijuana; and gave city governments the means to regulate dispensaries. While Proposition 215 made the medical marijuana industry legal, SB 420 made it legitimate.

Progressive cities like Oakland, Berkeley, and San Francisco had the most success in developing effective regulations. They were, in some cases, developed through trial and error, but mostly these cities struck working balances between the industry, conflicting legal issues, and community sensibilities. According to the ASA, more than 40 California cities and counties have enacted medical marijuana ordinances.[8] As in most cities, ordinances in Santa Barbara, West Hollywood, and Sebastopol were not accompanied by increases in crime. In some cases, tight security around dispensaries had the effect of reducing it. But an estimated 129 municipalities, 17 of them in Orange County, enacted dispensary bans. As this book went to press, a pending lawsuit in Anaheim would determine whether municipal governments had the authority to ban dispensaries. The case was being closely watched by law enforcement agencies, city councils, and medical marijuana advocates.

The ban on dispensaries, of course, did not mean these cities had banned marijuana. It simply meant local governments had relegated its control and distribution to the underground economy. In those towns that did regulate medical marijuana, the marketplace's profit-driven discipline has helped corral the outlaw ethos that once dominated the marijuana black market. In California, dispensary owners have often become upstanding members of their communities. It is not unusual for dispensary owners to belong to their local chambers of commerce, and some contribute to political campaigns, beautification projects, and Little League teams. Cities that seemed to have the most difficulty with the medical marijuana industry either avoided regulating the dispensaries or were locked in internal disagreement over how to regulate them.

In some cases, dispensaries opened in cities that didn't have ordinances, and local elected officials have chosen to avoid regulating them for a number of reasons. One is they worry about being depicted as soft on drugs. Another is some towns simply don't have the resources to assign a deputy city attorney to wade through the state's confusing labyrinth of laws, policies, and guidelines. What exactly should health department officials look for during inspections? How do local officials know if dispensaries are selling marijuana contaminated with pesticides or mold? What parts of town should dispensaries operate in? How do cities assure no shady characters are involved in the medical marijuana business? Can a dispensary be insured? How much security should be required? Should security guards get background checks?

Going National

While California's cities and counties experimented with a new industry and the state legislature tinkered with its new law, other states were watching. By 1998, Alaska, Washington, and Oregon (the first state to decriminalize marijuana, in 1973) had approved their own versions of medical marijuana laws. In 1999, Maine was the first non-Western state to approve such a ballot measure, and over the next decade, Hawaii, Colorado, Montana, Nevada, New Mexico, New Jersey, Rhode Island, and Vermont all had working medical marijuana laws. In all, 27 percent of the American population lived in states covered by those laws. Nine of those states were in the west. *Newsweek* estimated a total of 369,634 medical marijuana users nationwide. California had 253,800 users, or 69 percent of the total, though it was only a rough estimate because California registration is voluntary.

All but two states allowed patients to cultivate marijuana in their homes. The exceptions were New Jersey, which is generally considered to have one of the strictest laws, and New Mexico, which required a special license to cultivate. Five states—Maine, New Jersey, New Mexico, Rhode Island, and Vermont—created their laws through legislative acts; the laws in the other nine states were voter approved. After California approved Proposition 215, every such state ballot measure won except in South Dakota, where an initiative failed in 2006.

In each state, the medical marijuana industry has taken a different shape, thereby creating interesting themes and variations.

Colorado

Colorado voters approved Amendment 20 in 2000 with 54 percent of the vote. But the amendment, like California's Proposition 215, was vague. Amendment 20 allowed physicians to authorize medical marijuana licenses to patients and caregivers who could then grow, possess, and use cannabis. For several years afterward, marijuana patients were restricted to obtaining marijuana from designated caregivers, who could have no more than five clients. Then in 2007, a court struck down the limits on patients, and the medical marijuana business began to boom. By 2009, hundreds of dispensaries were operating around the state.

In February of that year, U.S. attorney general Eric Holder announced that the DEA would not prosecute medical marijuana caregivers, patients, or cultivators as long as they were in compliance with state law. The announcement triggered a second wave of new dispensaries. In Denver alone, an estimated 400 dispensaries were operating. So many had opened on South Broadway that the street was nicknamed "Broadsterdam." Another 100 dispensaries had also opened in nearby Boulder. With no permitting system in place, no one knew for sure what the exact count was.

Colorado's medical marijuana law lacked California's nonprofit or cooperative requirements. This difference helped fuel the Colorado green rush because investors, sometimes from out of state, were bankrolling new dispensaries. Law enforcement agencies became nervous because they had no way of tracking who was entering the state's marijuana business.

Residents in Denver and Boulder were alarmed at the number of dispensaries operating near schools. As Boulder's DA, Stanley Garnett was put in a tough spot. He was a supporter of medical marijuana, but as he struggled with the dispensary boom, medical marijuana advocates began attacking him. In a letter posted on a popular Boulder news blog, Garnett explained his position. "As district attorney for the 20th District, I am committed to having the most progressive approach to medical marijuana of any DA's office in the state," wrote Garnett. But he also offered examples of unanswered questions the city was facing. "Is large-scale commercial growing legal? We have received notice of an operator wanting to put a large grow in a warehouse across from a middle school in Longmont. Is this legal?"

Two months later, the Boulder City Council approved a set of temporary regulations designed to slow down the explosion of dispensaries. Worried that the council might ban dispensaries, more than 100 area residents crowded into the council chamber. But that wasn't the case. The council allowed 42 dispensaries that had taken out sales-tax licenses to remain in business. It didn't ban new dispensaries, but restricted them from opening near schools. Within several months of passing the temporary regulations, the city of Boulder had collected $74,000 in dispensary sales tax revenue. The Denver City Council also approved temporary regulations that required dispensaries to submit floor and security plans. For each dispensary, the cost of the various licenses, sales tax license, zoning permit, and burglar alarm license fee topped $5,000.

As in California, Amendment 20 put the dispensaries in conflict with existing anti-marijuana laws. Denver Councilman Charlie Brown, who proposed the ordinance, said crafting it was "like trying to pick your teeth with a rattlesnake." In 2009, Senator Chris Romer, who represents Denver, submitted House Bill 1284, which he wrote to create overarching state law to govern the booming medical marijuana industry. The bill was immediately controversial. Medical marijuana advocates and Colorado's new class of businessmen were convinced Romer wanted to shut down the dispensaries, and rumors began to fly. One was that HB 1284 would create a $50,000 annual license fee. Another was it would allow warrantless searches of dispensaries and require dispensary operators to turn over patients' names. Another rumor was that dispensaries' books would be inspected every five days. None of these rumors were accurate, according to medical marijuana political consultant Matt Brown, executive director of Coloradans for Medical Marijuana Regulation, an advocacy group that sought regulations for dispensaries to legitimize the industry.

But Romer, the son of former governor Roy Romer, caused trouble for the bill when he was videotaped saying it would close 50 percent of Colorado's dispensaries, and that "auditors with guns" would inspect those that remained every few days. The catchy phrase caught on like wildfire among medical marijuana advocates, who were hostile to increased regulations.

At the time this book went to press, the Colorado State Senate had approved Romer's 60-page bill and it was headed to the House for final approval. Once law, the bill would require background checks for dispensary owners as well as examination of their funding sources to preclude criminal enterprises from investing in the state's medical marijuana industry. It seeks to gain some control over cultivation by requiring dispensaries to grow 70 percent of the marijuana they sell.

A new regulatory agency would be created, consisting of 27 enforcement agents, auditors, and administrators that would be paid for by the estimated $2 million in dispensary licensing and safety fees.

The bill also gives cities and counties the option to regulate the medical marijuana industry or simply ban it outright. Many local officials were happy with the provision because it gave them a sense of control over the issue. But advocates saw that as a recipe for trouble. "You have individuals who are city councilors and county commissioners who will invoke their personal biases against marijuana and shut it down," said Clifton Black, a Colorado Springs attorney who counsels medical marijuana industry clients. He added that the Colorado General Assembly was making local cities and counties vulnerable to the inevitable lawsuits that will be filed as soon as one bans dispensaries.

Montana

Montana voters approved Initiative 148 in 2004 with 62 percent of the vote. As in Colorado, its medical marijuana industry accelerated after Attorney General Holder's February announcement. The number of registered patients shot up from 2,000 to 12,000, and small-town elected officials grew nervous.

Initiative 148, like other legalization devices in other states, was vague. It didn't allow for dispensaries per se, but many caregivers were renting commercial space to grow medical marijuana—they can grow up to six plants per patient—and use a location to provide marijuana. These businesses, like Zoo Mountain Natural Care in downtown Missoula, are typically referred to as "enterprises." Initiative 148 was also silent on the cultivation of marijuana, and many of the enterprises have leased large warehouse space to grow for their patients. One of Zoo Mountain's owners, Logan Head, said Montana's medical marijuana law was challenging. "We are growing everything ourselves in a warehouse outside of Missoula," Head told a reporter. "It takes three months for a plant to mature, and that's a problem with supply. We are the only industry where we have to be in the whole supply chain from manufacturing to middleman, from seed to dispensing the supply."

Concerns among local officials and vagueness in Initiative 148 led the state legislature to form an interim committee to look at some of the holes in the law. Legislators hoped to amend the initiative so local jurisdictions knew what they could do to regulate the medical marijuana industry. They also wanted more clarity on whether enterprises should be inspected and whether or not caregivers were required to tell landlords the nature of their business.

Those in Montana's rural areas were concerned that tougher

laws might force caregivers out of the larger cities and into smaller towns. The concern was so great that in the town of Choteau, a small burg in the high plains of central Montana, the city council decided to take preemptive action. As the council discussed possible solutions, the small council chamber was packed with some of Choteau's 1,700 residents who opposed a proposal that would require caregivers to apply for a license and pay a fee. Finally, after a month of discussion, the council passed an ordinance that prevented caregivers from selling medical marijuana from cars or carts.[9]

In Billings, the state's largest city, things got a little rougher in May 2010. As the city council was preparing to vote on a proposed ban on medical marijuana enterprises, two businesses that provided cannabis were firebombed. In both cases suspects broke the front window and threw in a beer bottle filled with gasoline. Surveillance cameras showed two young men spray painting "not in our town" on the front of the business.

As in other states, Montana experienced the rapid growth of medical marijuana businesses, which exposed weaknesses in the law. And like in other states, Montana's state legislature is examining ways to control the industry.

Oregon

Oregon approved Ballot Measure 67 in 1998. The law was specifically designed to keep the medical marijuana industry from being taken over by profit-driven companies. The state has largely been successful at that, but the law hasn't been very popular. Patients have argued that the law made it difficult to arrange regular access to marijuana. The problem, some said, was that the law allows them to use and possess marijuana, but prohibits them from buying it other than to reimburse their caregivers.

Law enforcement has also been frustrated because the law doesn't give them the authority to inspect large-scale grow operations, many of which are in old barns and converted homes. Officers suspect that many of the operations present fire hazards or, in some cases, that the growers are illegally supplying the black market, but their hands are tied when it comes to investigating the grow sites. As the law stands, law enforcement officers cannot cross the threshold of a grow location if the occupant has a medical marijuana card.

Marijuana entrepreneurs are frustrated because they are prevented from operating dispensaries, which is where the serious money is made. Like many law enforcement officials, Senior Deputy District Attorney Mark McDonell favored a nonprofit dispensary model in which the growers were state licensed. That approach could reduce the number of unregulated grow operations, McDonell said. And it would give the law enforcement the legal tools to go after black-market growers. "If you have dispensaries, there's no reason to allow [unlicensed] growers," McDonnell said.

With just about everybody in Oregon ready for a change, two petitions were being passed around the state. The Oregon Regulated Medical Marijuana Supply System (also known as I28), would allow for nonprofit dispensaries, similar to California's, to operate in Oregon. This initiative was probably the most favored option by medical marijuana activists, patients, and law enforcement.

The other petition, the Oregon Cannabis Tax Act, would create a commission to oversee and license the legal retail sale of marijuana to adults, but anyone could grow marijuana without a medical marijuana card or other licensing. Oregon NORML pushed the legalization option, focusing support on its cultivation aspect, which they assessed as a weak spot in the prodispensary initiative. "I want to grow organic, and I don't want anyone taking that away from me," said Oregon NORML executive director Madeline Martinez. Similar initiatives have been put before Oregon voters in the past and have always failed.

Opposing both initiatives is Stormy Ray, a Salem resident who worked hard to pass Oregon's original medical marijuana initiative in 1998. Ray said both proposals would have a corrupting influence on medical marijuana. Currently marijuana patients pay about $40 per ounce for marijuana, which is what the legitimate caregivers charge. (The black market price is about $250 per ounce.) If the dispensaries in California or Colorado are any indication, medical marijuana patients in Oregon can expect higher prices if voters approve dispensaries. A quick review of California's dispensary Web sites shows "lowest price available" at around $500 an ounce. In Colorado, prices run about $375 an ounce.

Ray, who admits about one-third of medical marijuana patients have a hard time either growing their own or finding someone to supply them, said if voters approve dispensaries, something will be lost. "This program is about kindness," Ray said. "When you start registering stores, you take the ownership out of the patients' hands and put it into the hands of a third party that is only there to make money."

New Mexico

When New Mexico approved its medical marijuana law in 2007, it had a unique provision for cultivation. The law required the state to authorize growing operations—a bold move because state employees became vulnerable to federal arrest. Shortly after Governor Bill Richardson signed the bill, the Bush administration threatened to arrest state health department employees for implementing the new law. Richardson, who had announced his candidacy in the 2008 presidential primaries, publicly challenged the DEA to arrest him. "I say to the Bush people, don't arrest a poor $60,000-a-year researcher, arrest me," he said. "Come after me, because I pushed for this law."[10]

Federal Inertia

Congress had been very effective at outlawing marijuana in the '30s and '70s, but now is having difficulty reversing those laws, even though a vast majority of Americans support medical marijuana. Despite years of lobbying by nonprofits like NORML and the Marijuana Policy Project, Congress has refused to budge from what was increasingly an outdated stance on marijuana. Symbolic of that inertia is marijuana's status as a Schedule I narcotic, its designation since 1970, when the Controlled Substances Act was authorized under President Richard Nixon. That designation seemed outdated when it had been so widely used without significant levels of addiction or physical harm. Even crack cocaine was considered safer than marijuana, according to the Controlled Substances Act.

In recent years, marijuana's Schedule I status began to rankle the country's medical associations. In 2008, the American College of Physicians, the second largest physician's group, approved a resolution calling for an evidence-based review of marijuana's status as a Schedule I controlled substance. A year later, the American

Medical Association, the country's largest physician group, voted to reverse its position that marijuana remain on the list. An AMA science council had determined that marijuana reduced neuropathic pain, improved appetite and caloric intake—particularly in patients with reduced muscle mass—and that it may relieve spasticity and pain in multiple sclerosis patients. The AMA resolution also called for clinical research with the goal of developing cannabinoid medicines. "The two largest physician groups in the U.S. have established medical marijuana as a health care issue that must be addressed," ASA government affairs director Caren Woodson said. "Both organizations have underscored the need for change by placing patients above politics."

Congress has been just as recalcitrant when it comes to prohibition. Two U.S. representatives have repeatedly tried to prevent federal agencies from meddling with legalized medical marijuana. Dana Rohrabacher, an Orange County Republican who represents one of the most conservative districts in California, and New York Democrat Maurice Hinchey submitted a bill that would have defunded Department of Justice programs that interfered with medical marijuana activities in states where it was legal. Congress voted on the Hinchey-Rohrabacher Amendment five times between 2003 and 2007.[11] Although it was always defeated, it received between 148 and 165 votes, picking up a few each time.

In 2010, two medical marijuana bills were working their way through congressional subcommittees. Representative Barney Frank introduced the Medical Marijuana Patient Protection Act, which would allow the medical use of marijuana in states that had adopted medical marijuana laws. Frank's bill would also change marijuana from a Schedule I narcotic to a Schedule II. The other bill, the Truth in Trials Act, introduced by Sam Farr, would allow defendants facing federal marijuana charges to reveal to juries that their marijuana activity was medically related. The fact that medical marijuana patients, dispensary operators, and cultivators have not been allowed to introduce evidence of their state-sanctioned medical status has been a major bone of contention among medical marijuana defendants, lawyers, and advocates.

A poignant example of how the people are ahead of their leaders when it comes to medical marijuana occurred in Washington, DC. The city that hosts the White House, the U.S. Capitol, and the Washington Monument, has legalized medical marijuana. Voters first passed the measure in 1998 with 69 percent of the vote, but Republican congressman Bob Barr was able to hold up its implementation for 12 years, first by refusing to provide funds to count the votes, and later by blocking DC from spending money to implement the medical marijuana measure.

Ironically, Barr, who was voted out of office in 2003, became a lobbyist for his former nemesis, the Medical Marijuana Project, in 2007 after rethinking his stance.

While Congress stood pat on medical marijuana issues, states were proceeding with legislation. In 2010, 11 more states had medical marijuana bills or ballot measures in progress. Meanwhile, a new breed of activists had organized to confront federal, state, and local resistance to medical marijuana.

California and the DEA

In 2002, a series of DEA raids in Oakland revealed a shared characteristic between the medical marijuana industry and the plant itself: both seemed to thrive under harsh conditions. The harder the DEA tried to suppress the industry, the stronger it became. In fact, the DEA raids in 2002 triggered a wave of organized activism that has not relented since.

In February 2002, DEA agents raided the Oakland home of cultivation icon Ed Rosenthal. They confiscated 100 plants that he was growing for the Harm Reduction Center, a dispensary in San Francisco. Rosenthal, an avuncular horticulturalist, author, columnist, and publisher, had written more than a dozen books on marijuana cultivation, including *Marijuana Growing Tips* and *Marijuana Grower's Guide*. His cultivation skills were so respected that the city of Oakland had deputized Rosenthal in 1998 to grow marijuana for medical purposes. Rosenthal wrote the popular "Ask Ed" column for *High Times* and *Cannabis Culture* magazines, and also owned Quick Trading Company, which published marijuana-oriented books and calendars.

Rosenthal's arrest sent shockwaves through the medical marijuana community. The following day, activist and organizer Steph Sherer was alarmed to see local newspapers had barely covered the arrest. She called a meeting of the Berkeley Patients Group, an activist-based dispensary that had opened in 2000. Sherer held up a copy of the *San Francisco Chronicle* showing the assembled group that the story of Rosenthal's arrest had been buried.

Don Duncan, the dispensary's cofounder, recalled the meeting. "When those raids happened, it was a wake-up call to how fragile our movement was," Duncan said. "Ed was one of our figureheads, and the newspaper story was buried way in the back of the first section. Everyone agreed that something had to be done to call more attention to Rosenthal's arrest, so we formed this temporary organization, Americans for Safe Access, just for this one media campaign." They chose the name for its acronym, ASA, which was meant to mock U.S. attorney general Asa Hutchinson, who had scheduled a trip to San Francisco to crow about the recent raids. "We were thinking it would be 'ASA vs. Asa,'" Duncan said.

Rosenthal was convicted in 2003 on charges of felony conspiracy and cultivation. But U.S. district court judge Charles Breyer sentenced him to only one day in jail, which he had already served.

Instead of disbanding the ASA after Hutchinson's visit, organizers realized they had created a valuable tool. They redoubled their media efforts and expanded the scope of their advocacy. By 2007, the ASA had organized court support for more than 30 medical marijuana defendants facing federal charges. It had also conducted a 26-city training tour designed to educate dispensary owners and patients on their legal rights.[12]

With a budget of about $1.5 million, the ASA now has more than 30,000 members in 40 states and is headquartered in Washington, DC, where it lobbies for federal legislation. Sherer is its executive director, and Duncan directs the California office, which is based in Oaksterdam. Unlike other marijuana advocacy groups, the ASA doesn't take positions on political campaigns or lobby for the legalization of adult use. Instead, it focuses strictly on advocating for the medical marijuana industry and patients' rights.

The ASA has developed a reputation for scrappy, grassroots activism. In fact, the organization has a preparedness policy that requires its chapters be ready at all times to respond to DEA raids with placards, blow horns, and media spokespeople. In March 2009, the DEA raided Emmalyn's California Cannabis Clinic on Howard Street. Almost as soon as agents entered the dispensary, a text alert went out to ASA members. Within minutes, ASA members started to arrive, and soon there were two dozen people on hand to wave placards and chant "DEA go away" as the heavily armed agents loaded several vans with bins of plants, grow lights, and other cultivation equipment.[13]

ASA members often devote regular meetings to preparing materials and strategies in case of a raid. At a biweekly meeting of the San Francisco chapter at Bowzer's Pizza on 11th Street, about 20 volunteers discussed local medical marijuana court cases while nibbling on pizza. Afterward they broke out sheets of blank poster board, crayons, and coloring pens. The members cleared a space on the floor and began to write multicolored protest slogans on the stiff-backed paper such as "Change Is Inevitable," "I Need My Medicine," and "DEA GO AWAY!" ASA volunteers routinely carried materials for three or four placards in the trunks of their cars. Duncan, a veteran of many raid protests, always carries placard-making materials: a blow horn, energy bars, and bottled water in the trunk of his car. Other members carry digital cameras to record raids. Before the ASA's formation, DEA agents had a media advantage because they were the only source of information about their raids. But Duncan said the ASA took some of the DEA's advantage away by putting its members, many who are trained as spokespeople, at raid locations to talk to the media.

Deploying placards and protestors is only a small part of what the ASA does for the medical marijuana industry. The organization has worked with more than two dozen cities and counties to shape effective medical marijuana ordinances; lobbied U.S. lawmakers and legislative staff to block restrictions on medical cannabis; provided court support for 60 medical marijuana cases; and trained more than 600 public defenders on successful strategies for representing medical marijuana patients. It has also distributed patient-focused materials to 50,000 patients, conducted hundreds of trainings for more than 10,000 patients, and organized two dozen days of action to oppose federal policies. Its other accomplishments include a successful lawsuit compelling the California Highway Patrol, the largest law enforcement agency in the state, to stop confiscating cannabis if it was being transported for legiti-. mate medical marijuana dispensaries. It successfully sued the city of Emeryville in 2006 for destroying $15,000 of medical cannabis.

The arrest of Ed Rosenthal backfired on the DEA. It unintentionally caused the formation of a highly organized and motivated advocacy group that has probably done more to implement and protect Proposition 215 than all other organizations combined. "There was a tiny group of us in the Bay Area that was vigilant through the era when the movement could have been snuffed out." Duncan said. "Now there is a whole generation that has grown up with legal medical marijuana available, and the idea that there wouldn't be safe access is incomprehensible to them."

By 2004, Proposition 215 had been repeatedly challenged, and many of its leaders arrested, prosecuted, and, in some cases, imprisoned. But SB 420 was in place, the ASA had become a vigilant watchdog, and the medical marijuana industry was formalizing its presence through local regulation. And one city in particular was distinguishing itself as a model of success.

CHAPTER 4

An Industry Takes Shape

Perhaps more than any other city, Oakland had been at the vanguard of the medical marijuana industry. It forged workable regulations for the industry, established local taxation, and has begun to develop legislation that would allow it to oversee large-scale growing operations. Oakland cannabis workers were the first in the nation to unionize. By 2010, the medical marijuana industry as it existed in Oakland was very popular with city residents. The once-blighted Oaksterdam district was now bustling with activity and had become something of a tourist destination. The Oakland Police Department supported the industry without reservation, and the city's Harborside Health Center had become a media showcase for professionalism and sophistication.

Oakland had certain advantages over other cities. Its bureaucracy was smaller and more agile than the one in San Francisco, where sluggish layers of commissions, boards, and bickering supervisors often made change difficult. And compared to Berkeley, a smaller city with quiet neighborhoods and loud zoning debates, Oakland could more easily absorb dispensary activities. Many of Oakland's dispensary owners were former activists who were eager to help the city develop new regulations and even pay a special local tax if it would help make the industry legitimate.

Oakland city officials were equally eager to work with dispensary owners. Almost as soon as Proposition 215 passed, they got to work. "After the law's passage, the City of Oakland government came to us for advice," Jeff Jones said. "We became the known experts. We became the people the officials . . . looked to because we were downtown prior to the law passing, and they knew we were going to answer questions faster than their own bureaucratic arm."

Jones continued to operate the Oakland Cannabis Buyers' Cooperative, as it was now called, until the DEA filed a lawsuit against him in 1998. By that time, Jones was operating a storefront dispensary like Peron's with a staff of 30. The feds claimed that not only was Jones violating the Controlled Substance Act, but he was also distributing a drug that had not been approved by the Food and Drug Administration. Jones had been waiting for this battle. He challenged the lawsuit using the medical-necessity defense for the dispensary, just as Robert Randall had done for himself in 1976. He and his attorney Robert Raich took the case to the U.S. Supreme Court, where they ultimately lost in a seven-to-one decision in 2000.

The DEA won that round, but it was unable to stop dispensaries in Oakland. Each time the DEA shut down a dispensary, others would pop up to take its place. One of Jones's patients, who happened to be HIV positive, opened another dispensary up the street at 1735 Telegraph Avenue, which he called The Zoo. It was The Zoo's owner, Jones said, who coined the term "Oaksterdam" to refer to a roughly 10-block area in downtown Oakland that would become the first "Pot Town" in the country.

"He said 'This is going to be Oaksterdam, and we're not going to leave until they come and remove us,'" Jones recalled. "And it doesn't seem that they've been able to stop us."

During the first years after Proposition 215, activists with little or no business experience operated Oakland dispensaries. That changed for the first time in 2001 when 58-year-old Larry Kristich came to town. Little was known about Kristich's background other than he had been connected somehow to the gaming industry. Tall and balding, Kristich was mild mannered, according to Oaksterdam University president Richard Lee.

"He looked like your average middle-class white guy. There was no flash really," Lee said. "All anyone really knew about his background was what he told people, and that was he had experience running a cash business because he had been involved in the gambling business."

Kristich had no links to the medical marijuana movement and no particular affinity for it beyond the fact that it was making him a lot of money. Once he opened his dispensary at 1740 Telegraph Avenue, Kristich interacted little with other dispensary owners or medical marijuana activists. Instead, he concentrated on building the first medical marijuana empire.

Kristich called his club Compassionate Caregivers, but it was known around town as "The Third Floor." At street level, there was no indication there was a marijuana dispensary in the building besides the two security guards who checked identification at the front door. For a short time, the second floor had been leased to doctors who provided medical marijuana recommendations. But that didn't last long because Kristich thought it drew too much attention to the dispensary.[1]

On the third floor, Kristich offered a wide selection of products that included marijuana, plants, and THC-laced candy bars, cookies, and soft drinks. The business was successful and Kristich began to expand. He branched out to San Francisco, where he operated a club at 790 Tennessee Street, and then moved south to Bakersfield, West Hollywood, and finally San Diego.[2] Kristich organized his dispensaries according to a classic business model. Compassionate Caregivers had some 200 employees at its height and Kristich paid withholding taxes, Social Security, and unemployment. He paid sales taxes to the state and offered his employees health insurance.[3]

And business was good. When he was indicted in 2007, court documents indicate his dispensaries brought in $6.7 million in 2002, $24.6 million in 2003, and a whopping $37 million in 2004. But Kristich's empire began to topple when the Los Angeles Police Department raided his West Hollywood dispensary, nicknamed the Yellow House, in May 2005. They confiscated $300,000 in cash, 800 pounds of marijuana, and THC-laced edibles. Federal authorities seized most of Compassionate Caregivers' assets, and its other six outlets were eventually forced to close.[4] Kristich fled to Costa Rica, but shortly after his indictment in 2007, he returned to the United States and surrendered to authorities. In 2009, he pled guilty to one count of maintaining a drug-involved business and one count of money laundering.[5] He was sentenced to five years at Taft Correctional Institution in California, which brought to an end the five-year saga of the first corporate-style chain dispensary.

According to Lee, Kristich began his enterprise with no particular loyalty to the medical marijuana movement. But at some point, he went through a transformation. "I think the medical marijuana movement finally got the better of him," Lee said. "You can't talk to very sick people or watch an amputee hop up three flights of stairs for medicine for very long and not be affected by it."[6] As evidence of Kristich's change of heart, he put his own name on an Oakland dispensary permit. By signing his own name, he was putting himself at risk of arrest and prosecution. Lee said it was the act of an activist.

As Kristich was building his Compassionate Caregivers empire, the Oaksterdam neighborhood was also thriving. Despite frequent DEA raids, there were eight dispensaries in the neighborhood by 2003 as well as related businesses, which included the Four Seasons Hydroponics on Broadway next to the Oakland Cannabis Buyers Cooperative. The neighborhood had undergone an economic turnaround. Besides bringing hundreds of jobs to the neighborhood, medical marijuana also brought thousands of patients and international media attention, most of which was positive. Other business owners in the area were, for the most part, happy with the neighborhood's transformation. Many said the presence of the clubs and ancillary businesses made the neighborhood cleaner and safer.

"We love them, we love them," Mario Paceppi, owner of the Fat Cat Café, told a newspaper reporter in 2003. "Because there are more eyes out. When it was more desolate, there was all sorts of horrible stuff going on. That's the only thing pushing the economy down here."[7]

Randy Csongor, manager of Best Collateral pawnshop, agreed. "It hasn't caused any problems. No fights, no riots, no outbreaks. Nothing like that. It could be dressmakers over there, it wouldn't be any different," Csongor said.[8]

But some city leaders were nervous that the industry was too successful. A total of 14 dispensaries had opened citywide, and some communities were beginning to complain. Problems such as traffic, parking, and loitering were beginning to crop up—nothing major, but city leaders wanted to get a handle on it before things got out of control. Oakland had not yet adopted a medical marijuana ordinance, and that omission made it difficult to control dispensary activity.

Oakland mayor Jerry Brown asked city inspectors to investigate the industry and make suggestions on how it could best be regulated. "These things have just grown up without any great public fanfare, so obviously, this has to be looked at carefully," Brown said in 2003. "Californians are strongly in support of medical marijuana, compassionate aid to people who are truly sick. But the big question is, what is the proper method of distribution, and how should it be regulated?"[9]

Mayor Brown and city council members worked with dispensary owners and activists to put Measure Z on the ballot. It made the enforcement of marijuana laws the police department's lowest priority and required the city to regulate the industry. Before Measure Z, counties and cities had been reluctant to establish strict regulations, primarily because the DEA regarded the local management of dispensaries as collusion. The federal agency had threatened some local governments with legal action. Local politicians also worried that creating a permitting process would generate a paper trail that federal prosecutors could use as evidence against dispensary owners.

The measure had wide support from the Oakland City Council, the Alameda County Board of Supervisors, and Congresswoman Barbara Lee. The measure was also popular with city residents, who approved it by 65.2 percent of the vote. The new regulations strictly limited the number of dispensaries to four.

Most of the exiled dispensaries fled across the bay to San Francisco or into the unincorporated areas of Alameda County, both of which were still unregulated.

The city's collective dispensary revenue took a hit as well. A report to the Measure Z oversight committee claimed that dispensary revenue dropped from an estimated $26.2 million in 2004 to $5.5 million in 2006, which caused a correlating drop in sales and payroll taxes. But without a regulated vetting process, the dispensaries were essentially underground operations, and the city had no control over who operated them, what hours they were open, and where they were located. The city also had little recourse for dealing with irresponsible dispensary owners who created problems in their communities.

"It made no sense," said City Councilmember Rebecca Kaplan, who was elected in 2008. "Can you imagine a restaurant or café opening without permits? There would be no control over the public health, how employees were treated, or whether or not the restaurant was in an appropriate commercial space." [10]

But despite the initial pain, Oakland's groundbreaking cannabis regulations paid off. The owners of the remaining four dispensaries went through extensive background checks, and their facilities had to meet the highest standards of the city's zoning ordinance. In addition, the four dispensaries had to demonstrate a commitment not only to medical marijuana patients, but also to the communities in which they were operating. Dispensary managers sought input from their neighbors and worked hard to comply with their wishes. The four dispensaries became models for best practices and community involvement. Two in particular, Richard Lee's Bulldog Coffee Shop and Steve DeAngelo's Harborside Health Center, were frequently in the news. Harborside, with its tasteful interior, holistic approach to healing, and waterfront location, became a favorite of television news programs.

By working with the city, Oakland's dispensary owners created a model for regulation that other cities quickly copied. By 2005, more than 40 clubs were operating in San Francisco, and the medical marijuana industry was experiencing an antidispensary backlash. One club stirred up a minor controversy when it attempted to open in a hotel that was receiving a subsidy to house the homeless, many of whom were recovering from substance abuse problems.[11] South of Market residents complained about MendoHealing, a dispensary that reduced prices to $30 for an eighth of an ounce when the going price was $55. The result was long lines that wound out the front door and down the street. Similar complaints arose about the Green Door dispensary in the Mission District and three others that were clustered on the same street in the Sunset District.[12]

By the time San Francisco addressed the issue, it had become much more complicated than it had been in Oakland. San Francisco had more dispensaries, a greater diversity of political viewpoints, and differing opinions among elected officials on how to regulate the industry. Mayor Gavin Newsom called for a moratorium on new dispensaries until regulations could be put in place. Supervisor Ross Mirkarimi, whose district included Haight-Ashbury, took on the thankless task of writing the regulations.

Aaron Peskin, the former president of the Board of Supervisors, said Mirkarimi's task was not an enviable one. "With the vagueness of Proposition 215, the feds, and all the different opinions about what should be done, it was like a giant cluster fuck," Peskin said. "It would have been much easier if the industry had been organized under one cohesive monolith."[13]

Mirkarimi's regulations—which restricted dispensaries to certain neighborhoods, raised permit fees, and established a rigorous public approval process for new dispensaries—were ultimately adopted by a majority of the board. Unlike Oakland, San Francisco did not put a limit on the number of dispensaries. However, new zoning restrictions led to an overall reduction in the number of operating dispensaries. At its 2006 international conference, NORML presented Mirkarimi with the Rufus King Award for outstanding leadership in the reform of marijuana laws.

Like Oakland, Berkeley established a clear regulatory framework. Working closely with the dispensaries, the city put Measure JJ, or the 2008 Patients Access to Medical Cannabis Act, on the ballot. The resulting regulations took the extra step of creating the Berkeley Medical Cannabis Commission, which meets once a month to vet dispensary applications and monitor any community problems.[14] Other California cities, like Arcata, Santa Barbara, and Sebastopol, saw the positive impact regulating the industry and followed suit with good results.

In Oakland, the new regulations helped the cannabis-based businesses to thrive. The Oaksterdam district now has only two medical marijuana dispensaries instead of seven, but businesses associated with the medical marijuana industry have continued to flock to the neighborhood: a Medicann medical clinic, a chain of medical offices that provides cannabis recommendations; the Patient ID Center (run by Jeff Jones), which provides medical cannabis identification cards; cannabis equipment and cultivation classes; ASA's California headquarters; OD Media, a marketing company that specializes in the cannabis business; and several law offices that specialize in medical marijuana law. And noncannabis businesses, particularly restaurants, moved into the neighborhood hoping to capitalize on the foot traffic generated by the dispensaries. Oaksterdam was not only safer than it had been prior to the medical marijuana industry moving in, but it had become something of a tourist attraction, which is evidenced by the Oaksterdam Gift Shop on 15th Street.

Higher Education

In 2007, the national media returned to Oakland when the first cannabis industry trade school opened. Oaksterdam University offered an array of classes to train students in every facet of the industry: cultivation, dispensary operation, cooking, cannabis law, cannabis history, cannabis science, cannabis business and economics, and the critical importance of political activism. All classes emphasized the importance of professional practices and forming strong working relationships with the community. The university's immediate success forced it to move three times to accommodate its growing roster of students. In 2010, the Oakland campus moved to a four-story, 30,000-square-foot building.

At 48 years old, Oaksterdam University's founder and president Richard Lee had a youthful appearance, which belied the fact that he was quickly becoming one of the industry's most influential leaders. Born in Houston to a conservative Republican family, Lee majored in advertising and public relations at the University of Houston. In 1991, he was the victim of a violent carjacking that changed his perception of law enforcement. Flung from the wheelchair he has used since a spinal cord injury in his youth, Lee was left sprawled on the street for 45 minutes before police officers arrived. The officers didn't call an ambulance, and when

Lee asked for a ride home, they curtly told him they weren't a taxi service. The incident convinced Lee that the police should focus on violent criminals, not marijuana users.

In 1992, Lee cofounded Legal Marijuana, The Hemp Store in Houston, one of the first hemp retail businesses to open in the United States.[15] He moved to the West Coast in 1997, a year after voters approved Proposition 215. He had originally planned to move to San Francisco, but there was an opportunity to work for Ed Rosenthal's Quick Trading Company, a well-known training ground for careers in the marijuana industry. Lee was an avid reader of Rosenthal's books, which inspired him to pursue his entrepreneurial instincts. In 1997, he cofounded the Hemp Research Company, which grew cannabis for the Oakland Cannabis Buyer's Club. The company also developed efficient and safe horticulture techniques.[16] In 1999, Lee started the Bulldog Coffee Shop, an Amsterdam-style cannabis café.

"I am so happy that I wound up in Oakland," Lee said, sitting on a couch in the university's executive offices. "It's really like a small town, which fits my upbringing in the south. San Francisco is too much like New York, and in many ways Oakland is more progressive than both San Francisco and Berkeley." His own politics, Lee said, are more libertarian. In 2003, he founded the Oakland Civil Liberties Alliance, which became the engine behind the 2004 passage of the influential Measure Z.

After visiting a cannabis college in Amsterdam, Lee wanted to found a similar institution. In 2007, he placed an ad for a cannabis trade school in the *East Bay Express*, an alternative weekly, and received more than 200 responses the first week. Lee quickly organized his first class of 20 students in a small rented classroom on 15th Street. An intrigued national media generated a tsunami of press and inextricably linked Lee's boyish face with the medical marijuana industry.

In 2009, Lee and other Oakland dispensary owners again worked with city officials to qualify Measure F for the ballot, which would quadruple the amount of taxes dispensaries paid. Oakland dispensaries had been paying the same sales tax rate as other retail businesses. The annual tax was $60 for the first $50,000 in revenue and $1.20 for each $1,000 earned after that. Measure F would raise the tax on dispensaries to $18 for each $1,000 earned. The new tax was expected to generate $294,000 in 2010, its first year. No opposing arguments against the new tax were filed, and Oakland voters approved Measure F with 80 percent of the vote.[17] Similar tax measures were proposed in other cities, and state and federal politicians began to look at the medical marijuana business in an entirely new light.

With the industry's new tax status came more political and legal security. The ordinance was irrefutable proof that the industry was willing to contribute to the community. The new law also energized local and national level efforts to legalize marijuana. "This tax is just one of many. It's one battle in a big war," Lee told the *Sacramento Bee*. "It's a reverse tax revolt: No taxation without legalization."[18]

Thanks to the efforts of progressive elected officials and community-minded dispensary owners, the medical marijuana industry was increasingly interwoven into civic life. And with each new regulation, each new emblem of legitimacy, the political movement more closely resembled an ordinary commercial enterprise.

In the spring of 2010, Oakland yet again broke new ground for the industry. About 100 cannabis workers voted to join the

United Food and Commercial Workers Local 5. By joining the 26,000-member union, employees at six marijuana-related businesses, including Oaksterdam University, the Bull Dog Café, and the Oaksterdam Gift Shop, had added another layer of legitimacy to the medical marijuana industry. Membership in the union would give the industry more influence with elected officials and business associations, as well as in political campaigns.

Meanwhile, across the bay, San Francisco's ordinance helped legitimize the industry, but it was also the death knell for the dispensary where Peron had illegally opened the Cannabis Buyers' Club on Church Street in 1994. Ironically, the new ordinance forced the dispensary, with which Peron was no longer involved, to close because it didn't meet the new requirement for wheelchair access. The closure was another symbol of the industry taking precedence over its founding political movement.

CHAPTER 5

Growing Pains

Los Angeles Councilman Dennis Zine is an imposing man. A police officer for 41 years, he still has the bearing of a tough, no-nonsense cop with a vague resemblance to Telly Savalas. Like many large men, Zine softens his imposing presence with a degree of warmth and a ready sense of humor. On a fall day in 2009, he strode into his office conference room, where I was waiting to interview him. Without a greeting, he reached into his briefcase and removed a three-inch troll doll with flaming red hair and plopped it on the table in front of me. The plastic toy suddenly emitted a tinny recording of a raucous laugh. "That's what I think of the medical marijuana situation in Los Angeles," Zine said.

Despite the whimsy, Zine was defensive. In May 2005, there were only four dispensaries operating in Los Angeles, and Zine was the one councilman who foresaw the need to regulate them. He began pushing the 15-member city council to craft an ordinance, but more than four years later, council members were still bickering among themselves and with the city attorney's office. As a result, dispensaries opened without licenses or inspections and operated near schools, playgrounds, senior centers, and in crime-ridden neighborhoods. Alarmed business owners, school officials, and community organizations inundated the council with complaints about traffic, loitering, and public pot smoking. The situation intensified in February 2009, when U.S. attorney general Eric Holder said the DEA would no longer raid dispensaries operating in accordance with state law. The announcement accelerated the city's green rush, and the local media began to criticize the council for years of dithering while the situation spun out of control. *Newsweek* called Los Angeles the "Wild West of Weed."[1]

Zine was no great supporter of medical marijuana, but he understood a good ordinance would give the city some control over where dispensaries opened and how they operated. On the day I interviewed him, he was upset about a story that was about to be published in the *LA Weekly*. The story headline would be "L.A.'s Medical-Weed Wars: How the Potheads Outwitted [Mayor] Antonio Villaraigosa and the L.A. City Council."[2] The story unfairly suggested Zine had come under the Svengali-like influence of a medical marijuana advocate. Zine was unhappy with the portrayal, which seemed to bring out the councilman's tough cop persona. Now he was making sure the proposed ordinance wouldn't be too permissive.

"We will go strictly by Proposition 215, and that's what we're going to do," he said using the point of his finger to rhythmically emphasize each point. "You're not going to be able to mask illegal drug operations as dispensaries. I'm sure there are people who want to do that, but they will suffer the consequences. We will take their goods. We will take their money. We will shut them down."

Zine had found himself in an increasingly common predicament among California politicians. Many do not support medical marijuana, but they realize the most effective way to prevent dispensary problems is to regulate them. The catch is it's nearly impossible for an elected official to advocate for regulations without tacitly accepting the existence of the medical marijuana industry. And that acceptance brings political risk. In some California cities, even those with overwhelming support for medical marijuana, elected officials avoid the issue at all costs. Fearful of political repercussions from either side of the issue, they support neither bans nor regulation. In some cases, that inaction can mean chaos, and no city fits that description better than Los Angeles.

Los Angeles's regulatory paralysis is more amazing when one considers the city's long cultural association with marijuana. It crops up as early as 1940 in Raymond Chandler's *Farewell My Lovely*. Eight years later, marijuana made headlines when movie star Robert Mitchum was convicted of possession; *Life* magazine ran a picture of him in prison garb mopping a floor. Mitchum's arrest was the inspiration for the 1949 anti-marijuana movie *She Should Have Said No*, which was also released as *Marijuana, the Devil's Weed*.[13]

Since the 1960s, recreational marijuana use has been a staple in Hollywood movies. The shift away from the industry's earlier anti-marijuana films can be found in the 1968 release of *I Love You, Alice B. Toklas*. Los Angeles attorney Harold Fine, played by Peter Sellers, mistakenly eats brownies filled with marijuana. The experience causes him to give up his conventional life and sends him on a comical search for the meaning of life. The landmark 1969 film *Easy Rider* depicts an extended scene of a pot-fueled discussion of aliens infiltrating American society. Dozens of stoner movies followed, including a series of Cheech and Chong films produced between 1978 and 1985. Those were followed by *Fast Times at Ridgemont High*, *The Big Lebowski*, and *Pineapple Express*, a 2008 film that was entirely pot-driven.

Nor did Los Angeles's music industry neglect marijuana. Recording artists and industry executives consumed more than their share during the 1960s and 1970s, and in 1992, Dr. Dre named his debut album *The Chronic*, street slang for high-grade marijuana. Dre's colleague, Snoop Dogg, has cultivated a public image of being perpetually stoned.

Besides the entertainment industry, Los Angeles is home to a thriving, pot-friendly art scene. In recent years the city has attracted large numbers of painters, sculptors, and installation and graphic artists who are drawn to Los Angeles for its affordable rent and creative communities. There are established artist enclaves in Chinatown, the downtown area, and Culver City. Santa Monica boasts one of the largest complexes of art studios and galleries in the state at the eight-acre Burgamot Station, a former trolley car barn. Los Angeles is also the spiritual homeland of the storied California Dream. For generations, beach bums, attorneys, accountants, and movie stars have emulated the surfer's ethos of sun worship and a laid-back approach to life that is consistent with smoking pot.

Cannabis was so deeply ingrained in Los Angeles's culture, that when the city's voters approved Proposition 215 by 56 percent—one of the highest margins in the state—no one was surprised. Nine years later, only four storefront dispensaries were operating in Los Angeles, one each in Hancock Park, Van Nuys, Rancho Park, and Cheviot Hills.

But when Zine called for a medical marijuana ordinance in

2005, the city council, the city attorney's office, and Mayor Antonio Villaraigosa fell into hysterical paralysis. While Zine had some support from other council members, he got none from the city attorney or Villaraigosa, whose stance on the issue was no stance at all. Villaraigosa, who was once a rising star of the California Democratic Party, had a policy of not addressing the issue publicly and behind the scenes practiced a Hamlet-like inaction when it came to the developing medical marijuana industry.[4] The council's sluggishness was perhaps even more remarkable considering its members were the highest paid in the United States, at $178,800 annually.[5]

Council members wasted months nitpicking and obstructing good faith efforts to create a workable ordinance. City Attorney Rocky Delgadillo, who opposed medical marijuana, began a pattern of delay almost from the beginning. For more than a year, he quibbled over wording with the city's planning committee. During that time, the number of dispensaries jumped to 98. And when the council finally approved a temporary moratorium, it contained a colossal loophole. Deputy city attorney Jeri Burge, who worked for Delgadillo, had insisted a hardship exemption be included, and it didn't take long for aspiring dispensary entrepreneurs to exploit it.[6]

In the first wave of applications, dispensaries seemed to be casting about for specific hardships. But in December 2008, attorney Stewart Richlin came up with a new and more sweeping rationale. Representing a host of dispensary owners, Richlin claimed in one of his applications that the owners had been forced to open their dispensary without city approval because registering would require them to confess to a federal crime. He also argued registering would make dispensaries vulnerable to federal raids, and that drug enforcement agents had systematically created a climate of terror and fear.[7] Other dispensary owners followed Richlin's lead. When the city council enacted the moratorium in 2007, 186 dispensaries were given temporary exemptions because they had submitted their applications before the deadline. But the city was receiving an average of six hardship applications a day, and dispensaries continued to open at will.

Instead of reining in dispensaries, the poorly crafted moratorium turned Los Angeles into a medical marijuana boomtown. Within two years of the moratorium's effective date, more than 800 dispensaries were operating in Los Angeles.[8] They opened in upscale business districts; near schools, playgrounds, and youth centers; and in high-crime neighborhoods. And without an ordinance requiring a criminal background check, many observers wondered whether some dispensaries were little more than covers for illicit drug dealing. According to a report prepared by LAPD narcotics detective Dennis Packer, numerous dispensaries had been robbed despite elaborate security precautions. In fact, the report claimed, some dispensaries hired gang members with long criminal histories as security guards.[9]

By 2009, medical marijuana dispensaries in Los Angeles outnumbered Starbucks or McDonald's franchises. Their ubiquity drew an embarrassing parallel to the fast food industry when the Kind For Cures dispensary leased a vacant Kentucky Fried Chicken outlet in Palms. A photograph of Kind For Cures (KFC) first ran on the *LA Weekly* blog, and it quickly became a minor Internet sensation. With its acronym sprawled in bright green letters, the dispensary seemed to mock the city for creating medical marijuana anarchy.[10]

Cracking Down

In May 2009, Carmen Trutanich was elected the new city attorney. Trutanich promised to crack down on dispensaries and quickly aligned himself with Los Angeles County District Attorney Steve Cooley. Both Cooley and Trutanich attended a training luncheon of state narcotics officers titled "The Eradication of Medical Marijuana Dispensaries in the City of Los Angeles and Los Angeles County." During a break in the training, Cooley held a press conference and told reporters that he was taking aim at all dispensaries that sell medical marijuana over the counter. "About 100 percent of the dispensaries in Los Angeles County and the city are operating illegally," Cooley said. "The time is right to deal with this problem."[11]

Cooley and Trutanich's hard-line position was a blow to the dispensary owners, patients' rights groups, and advocates who had been dutifully attending council and committee meetings for years. But it resonated with neighborhood groups, who were upset with the proliferation of dispensaries. They particularly expressed outrage over dispensaries opening near schools, playgrounds, and youth centers. And among some neighborhood councils, there was disenchantment with the widespread abuse of medical marijuana laws by recreational users. For these neighbors, the opportunity to thoughtfully manage a burgeoning industry was over.

The city's embarrassment continued in October 2009, when superior court judge James C. Chalfant ruled in favor of a dispensary owner who sued the Los Angeles for illegally extending the moratorium while it continued to struggle with an ordinance. The ruling added to the impression that city officials were at a loss when it came to controlling dispensaries. Robert Kahn, the dispensary owner's attorney, asked, "The Compassionate Use Act was passed in 1996. What have they been doing for the last 13 years?"[12]

Months before Judge Chalfant's ruling, about a dozen dispensaries opened along Pico Boulevard between La Cienega Boulevard and La Brea Avenue without permits. They advertised their presence with neon marijuana leaves on their green-painted façades. The dispensaries were typically locked and barred, and had numerous surveillance cameras protruding from the front of the building. Their creepy atmosphere unnerved some medical marijuana patients. Judy Bowen, a retired talent agent, had a doctor's recommendation for medical marijuana to treat her autoimmune disorder. When a dispensary opened near her home, she visited it and was quickly disappointed. "I was shocked. The building was falling apart. There was a stained carpet, a ripped sofa, a thuggy-looking guy with what looked like the bulge of a gun under his shirt, and a pushy, shady-looking salesman," she said. "There were just four jars of marijuana buds. That's not what a dispensary is supposed to be.... I felt like I'd walked into an episode of 'The Wire.'"[13]

One of the public's main concerns about dispensaries arises from the misconception that they are crime magnets. Although dispensaries are robbed less often than liquor stores or banks, such robberies typically make big news. In October 2008, a botched robbery made headlines throughout the state. The La Brea Collective, located on La Brea Avenue near West 8th Street, is a relatively small storefront dispensary on a busy commercial street. The dispensary has a bunker-type façade with a large mirrored plate-glass window and a steel-reinforced front door. To gain entrance, dispensary customers must first slide their medical marijuana recommendation and identification through a narrow slot in the front door. One afternoon, four armed men rushed the front door as a customer was leaving. Noe Campos Gonzalez, the collective's 25-year-old unarmed security guard, confronted the four suspects, and a scuffle broke out. Gonzalez was knocked to the ground, and as the four men exited the dispensary empty-handed, one of them shot Gonzalez several times in what police described as an execution-style killing while he lay on the sidewalk. Three of the four suspects, later identified as members of the Rollin' 30s Harlem Crips gang, were arrested for the killing.

Gonzalez's murder increased the political pressure to control the city's medical marijuana dispensaries. Paul Reznick, president of the West Los Angeles Chamber of Commerce, expressed frustration with the lack of regulations and the shady dispensaries that had opened in business districts. "Community retailers don't need any more problems. In these economic times, it's hard enough to attract customers, and when you have a reputation for medical marijuana shops, nobody likes that. And when you have a shooting, it just makes things worse," he said. "The city has to make a high-profile effort to shut these places down to a level that's manageable."[14]

As the public became more agitated, city officials continued their attempts to hammer out a workable ordinance. One person they turned to for guidance was ASA's Don Duncan, whom Morley Safer of *60 Minutes* once described as an "elder statesman in the world of medical marijuana." Duncan, who grew up in Los Angeles, also owns the Los Angeles Patients and Caregivers Group, one of four medical marijuana dispensaries in West Hollywood.

According to Duncan, cities usually have two major concerns that must be overcome before an effective ordinance can be written. The first concern was protecting the public, and the second was protecting the city from federal prosecution. Polls showed a huge majority of Americans approve of marijuana for medical use, but that support weakened when a medical marijuana dispensary was proposed for a particular neighborhood. "The devil is always in the details," Duncan said. "There can be majority support, but when you talk about a dispensary in your neighborhood, it's a different story. People are most often worried about crime, and the primary concern of regulators is how to protect the community from harm, whether real or perceived."[15]

Duncan denied any statistical correlation between dispensaries and crime, and said in his experience, well-run, well-regulated dispensaries with visible security tended to reduce crime in their neighborhoods. As far as penalties, the federal government had never sanctioned any county or city that adopted medical marijuana regulations. "It's a debate we tend to have over and over again in the regulatory process," Duncan said. "But the wrong attitude to take is to try and push medical marijuana back underground or into the shadows where you give up having any control at all."

Duncan agreed with Trutanich that the dispensary problem was out of control in Los Angeles. But agreement ended there. While the city's sheer size posed its own problems, Duncan thought the main challenges were bureaucratic. Delgadillo and Trutanich were obstructive, Duncan said. "I think there could have been a more proactive approach. The task to write the regulations fell to the city attorney, and both Carmen Trutanich and his predecessor Rocky Delgadillo were opposed to regulating medical marijuana dispensaries," Duncan said. "Delgadillo tenured most of his senior staff, so Trutanich was getting much of the same advice, and one of the challenges for new DAs is dealing with old staff and what is sometimes bad advice."

In nearly all of the five drafts to come out of the city attorney's office, both Delgadillo and Trutanich wanted a strictly cooperative type of dispensary with no over-the-counter sales and an inventory of no more than five pounds of cannabis at any given time. Each dispensary would have to grow the cannabis it sold and never have more than 100 plants on the premises. Trutanich claimed that allowing dispensaries to operate like normal retail businesses was counter to the intent of Proposition 215 and also ran afoul of the state attorney general's guidelines, which described "dispensaries" as an illegal use. Duncan argued that the Trutanich model of dispensary did not exist in California, and that Trutanich's real intent was to preclude all dispensaries from operating in Los Angeles. "Both Trutanich and Delgadillo kept proposing this hypothetical communal garden model where patients join together and grow together," Duncan said. "But they were completely ignoring the fact that virtually every other city in California was providing medical marijuana through a storefront model. They kept trying to put a round peg in a square hole." Duncan said a better starting place for Los Angeles would have been the Los Angeles County ordinance, which was approved in 2006 and allowed storefront dispensaries to operate as nonprofits.

After Duncan spent months in a working group charged with making recommendations for the city ordinance, *LA Weekly* ran a feature story depicting him as a puppet master who controlled council members Ed Reyes and Dennis Zine. The article claimed Duncan had such behind-the-scenes influence that he was approving documents, was allowed special access to city officials, and was even using a city hall parking space. Duncan brushed off the characterizations as a misguided and sensationalized interpretation. The story also suggested that Duncan was a marijuana kingpin whose dispensary clientele looked suspiciously healthy.

Duncan admitted there was wide abuse of medical marijuana by recreational users, as is common with many pharmaceuticals, but he insisted his first and foremost concern had always been the medical marijuana patient. The media "seem to be critical of the fact that I am communicating the patients' message, and for my part, I am not apologetic for that," he said. "All of the insinuations are nonsense. It's a whack-a-mole mentality."

With little support from dispensary owners, patients, or medical marijuana advocates, the Los Angeles City Council finally approved an ordinance in January 2010, more than four and half years after it began the process. The new ordinance strongly reflected Trutanich's interpretation of state law, which did not allow dispensaries to profit from over-the-counter sales of medical marijuana and imposed tough restrictions on where dispensaries could operate. The ordinance appalled medical marijuana advocates, who criticized it as one of the harshest in the state. The zoning restrictions were so severe that it was questionable whether dispensaries could operate anywhere but isolated industrial parks. James Shaw, the director of a marijuana patients union, said simply, "It's a disaster for patients."[16]

The ordinance capped the number of dispensaries at 70, though exceptions would be made for approximately 150 dispensaries that were operating before the council enacted its flawed moratorium. The catch was they would have to comply with the ordinance's restrictive zoning requirements, which required dispensaries to be at least 1,000 feet away from other dispensaries as well as "sensitive sites," such schools, parks, libraries, and churches.

At the last minute, the council added another restriction that prevented dispensaries from operating across the street or alley from residential properties. That requirement eliminated nearly all of the city's commercial streets, such as Melrose Avenue and Pico and Ventura boulevards. Dispensary owners desperately sought commercial space, but the city attorney's office did not provide a map of legal locations, and the few areas where dispensaries could operate might lack available commercial space or affordable rents. The zoning restrictions meant dozens of dispensaries would eventually have to close their doors.

Villaraigosa and most city council members were pleased the ordinance was finally approved. Councilman Zine, who had called for regulations in 2005, was particularly relieved. "I knew we'd get here eventually; I just didn't think it would take so long," he said. "We're doing an ordinance that we believe is lawful and that we believe can withstand lawsuits. They've threatened lawsuits for many, many years, so whatever we did in an ordinance we were going to be sued."

Zine was right. By March, the ASA filed a lawsuit in Los Angeles County Superior Court. They were joined by the Venice Beach Care Center and Pure Life Alternative Wellness Center, two dispensaries that had been operating in Los Angeles for roughly five years. By April, nearly two dozen dispensaries had joined the suit. The 11-page suit claimed the ordinance violated state law, and the plaintiffs sought an injunction to prevent it from taking effect. They claimed the restrictions were too onerous and that the ordinance "severely restricts access to medical marijuana by effectively forcing plaintiffs, as well as the vast majority of collectives in the city, to close their doors." Yamileth Bolanos, the owner of the Pure Life Alternative Wellness Center, said, "We want to work with the city to comply with its regulations, but such unreasonable requirements make compliance impossible."[17]

Meanwhile Trutanich was filing lawsuits of his own. He sought to enjoin Hemp Factor V, a dispensary in the Eagle Rock district, from selling cannabis. The court granted the injunction, and Trutanich immediately filed three more suits against a dispensary in Venice and two others in South Los Angeles. The flurry of suits caused the ASA to threaten countersuits because, it argued, Trutanich was overstepping the new ordinance.[18]

The Los Angeles experience contrasted sharply with that of other cities and counties, where ordinances have struck working balances between the concerns of patients, dispensaries, residents, and the larger community. Ironically, the mess caused by official inaction became the justification for an especially restrictive ordinance, which no one expected would curb the sale of recreational marijuana near schools, playgrounds, libraries, churches, or residences. The marijuana black market in Los Angeles would continue as it had for generations. And on April 19, 2010, Los Angeles County district attorney Steve Cooley announced his candidacy for California attorney general.

CHAPTER 6

The New Professionals

For more than 80 years, Americans have debated the dangers of cannabis, but no one doubts its commercial appeal. And now the medical marijuana industry has arrived—with a swagger.

As the industry grew, it was evolving and adapting to the marketplace. Dispensary owners, growers, and nonprofits formed self-regulatory groups that would monitor the quality of crops and establish best practices to increase public confidence. The industry's maturation caught the attention of corporate professionals who saw ground-floor opportunities. The image of the marijuana industry was buttoning down, but the change had not been smooth. There were public relations setbacks, some of which were related to criminal activity, such as selling cannabis to minors or wholesaling large quantities to street dealers.

A more serious problem was occurring in U.S. parklands. For most domestic growers, a garden of 100 plants was considered large. But in recent years, Mexican gangs had planted "monster garden" farms in remote areas of parklands in California, Oregon, Washington, Wisconsin, and Texas. The gangs guarded their crop perimeters with mines and tree-perched guards armed with

AK-47s. Some left piles of garbage and used pesticides and animal poisons that befouled creeks and groundwater systems.[1] No one knew how much of their cannabis was sold at dispensaries, but the DEA had shifted its focus from smaller outdoor gardeners to the Mexican gang growers, who continued to be an image problem for the medical marijuana industry.

The most embarrassing setbacks for the industry, however, were dispensary owners who behaved like big-shot drug dealers rather than compassionate caregivers. It was well known in the medical cannabis industry that the DEA frowned upon dispensary owners who promoted their businesses on a large scale, flaunted their wealth, or took on the flamboyant characteristics of illicit drug dealers. Yet some dispensary owners couldn't resist the temptation.

In 2006, former construction worker Shon Squier was enjoying a great deal of success from his dispensary, the Local Patients Cooperative in Hayward, California. Each Monday morning, customers formed a long line outside of the Foothill Boulevard dispensary for the free promotional samples Squier handed out to the first 50 customers that came through the door. Promotions like that helped the Local Patients Cooperative develop one of the largest patient bases in the area. Other dispensary owners marveled at Squier's bold marketing tactics and began to refer to his dispensary as "Wal-Pot."[2] Squier hired a staff of 60 people to handle the high volume.

Some said the 34-year-old Squier was enjoying his success a little too much. He purchased a $1.5 million home in the Hayward hills that had breathtaking views of the San Francisco Bay. He bought expensive motorcycles and automobiles, including a Hummer and a late-model Mercedes-Benz. Squier was generous with the Hayward community that he had grown up in, but he wasn't subtle. He contributed $100,000 to a variety of local charities and openly supported the Hayward High School football team, which made some parents nervous. He also offered special discounts to veterans and people in wheelchairs.

Squier's showy lifestyle caught the attention of the DEA, and the agency raided the Local Patients Cooperative in 2006. At the time, DEA special agent Gordon Taylor clarified what the DEA thought of dispensary owners in general and flashy ones in particular. "These people will tell you they are just interested in the terminally ill," he told the *Los Angeles Times*. "But what they are really interested in is lining their pockets with illegal drug money. When you pull the mask off, you see that they are nothing more than common dope dealers."[3]

Just a half block from Squier's marijuana emporium was another dispensary, the Hayward Patients Resource Center, which the DEA left alone. One reason was probably the low profile of its owner, Tom Lemos. "I live in a rental apartment and drive an '86 Isuzu with 245,000 miles on it," he told a newspaper reporter in 2007. When he appeared before the Hayward City Council, he prefaced his soft-spoken comment with "I don't live in a large house. . . ."[4]

Lemos's approach to a controversial business with a complex legal status seems like common sense. But common sense doesn't always prevail, as it didn't in the case of Luke Scarmazzo, a young dispensary owner whose name can cause law enforcement officers and dispensary owners alike to shake their heads.

In 2005, Scarmazzo opened a dispensary across the street from the Elks Lodge in Modesto, California, the sixth largest city in the state and the setting for George Lucas's *American Graffiti*.

Scarmazzo's background didn't recommend him as a conscientious young medical professional. In 2003, he and two friends attacked several teenagers who had thrown eggs at their car, and one of the teenagers died from multiple stab wounds to his buttocks and head.[5] Scarmazzo's friends pled guilty to manslaughter and received 15-year sentences. Scarmazzo pled guilty to assault, for which he received a time-served sentence of 16 months.

Not long after his release, Scarmazzo became involved with the California Healthcare Collective, which was located three blocks from the site of the homicide. According to federal prosecutors, California Healthcare Collective became the most successful dispensary in the entire Central Valley with revenues of more than $4.5 million in less than two years. Scarmazzo began to cultivate the persona of a street drug dealer. He wore gang-type clothing, went by the nickname "Kraz," and tooled around town in an $180,000 Mercedes-Benz.

Scarmazzo's trouble began when he indulged a longtime dream to become a hip-hop artist. He used his marijuana income to produce an elaborate video for his song, "Kraz-Business Man." The video starts with Scarmazzo wearing a business suit and addressing a city council. When a council member asks Scarmazzo "So, what are you really?" he breaks into rap about being a "business man." Later in the video, Scarmazzo is accompanied by bodyguards as he is chauffeured around downtown San Francisco in a caravan of Cadillac Escalades. The video cuts to Scarmazzo in a living room, now wearing a wife-beater T-shirt, surrounded by shady-looking thugs while he uses a bill counter to tally piles of cash. He puts the money in a cardboard box, which he has trouble finding space for in a back room that is crowded with stacks of other boxes—presumably all filled with cash.

The video exalts nearly all of the preconceptions the medical cannabis industry has struggled to overcome. While sneering into the camera, Scarmazzo describes himself as "rap's Ted Turner" who is irresistible to women. More disturbing, Scarmazzo repeatedly makes references to gunplay and violence. While pulling the trigger on imaginary handguns, Scarmazzo raps lyrics like "If you try to get me, I'll light your ass up," "Leaving fat snitches in ICU, and the next time I see you, you better cut like Ginsu," and "Many men wish death upon me, so I ride around these streets with a weapon on me representing M.O.D.E.S.T.O." One line in particular brought a great deal of attention to Scarmazzo, though it was probably not the kind of attention he had in mind. At one point, he flips off the camera with both hands and he raps "Put your fingers in the air and yell 'Fuck the feds.'"[6]

Scarmazzo posted the video on YouTube, where DEA agents saw it. In September 2006, a coalition of federal and local law agencies raided the California Healthcare Collective and seven private homes. Officers confiscated 65 pounds of processed marijuana, 34 pounds of cannabis-laced baked goods, 39 cannabis plants, $93,000 in cash, Scarmazzo's Mercedes-Benz, and five guns, two of which were stolen. DEA agents were investigating California Healthcare Collective before they saw the video, but they were certainly more motivated afterward. Federal prosecutors filed charges of manufacturing and distributing marijuana against Scarmazzo and his business partner, Ricardo Ruiz Montes. Federal DEA attorneys added a count for operating a continuing criminal enterprise, which carried a 20-year minimum sentence and was usually reserved for the most dangerous racketeering operations.

The video was the most sensational element in the trial, and prosecutors and defense attorneys played it repeatedly for jurors.

Scarmazzo testified the video was simply his way of expressing the view that the federal government was uncompassionate to ill people and was "turning a blind eye" to the medicinal benefits of marijuana. But jurors weren't convinced. After deliberating for two days, they came back with verdicts of guilty on all counts except a weapons charge. The two men received sentences of 21 years and 10 months.

Despite Scarmazzo's antics, the stiff sentence stunned many in the medical cannabis community. Several said it was evidence of how vindictive the DEA can be. After the verdict was read, Scarmazzo's attorney, Anthony Capozzi, told the *Modesto Bee* (May 16, 2008) that the sentence was unfair and suggested that the court had been particularly hard on Scarmazzo because of the video, which he admitted challenged the DEA's authority.

The New Professional

Yet for all the headlines, dispensary owners like Scarmazzo were increasingly rare. In fact, a new generation of professionals was flocking to the medical marijuana industry from successful careers in science, corporate America, and the ministry. By taking prominent jobs as lobbyists, managers, teachers, and nonprofit fundraisers, they were helping to mainstream the industry's image.

There's something enticing about a new industry. The air is charged with possibility, and as the new concept gains momentum, barriers that once seemed insurmountable are overtaken with breathtaking speed. The cannabis industry was crackling with that kind of excitement. Things were happening so fast, Oaksterdam University president Richard Lee observed, there was no time to consider which events will have historic importance. "I keep looking around my office and thinking I should save documents or items of furniture for a museum or something," Lee said. "But there just isn't any time."

Two newcomers were scientists Dr. Robert Martin and Dr. John Oram, who gave up traditional laboratory research for the exciting new world of marijuana. Martin, who holds graduate degrees in botany and mycology, was a professor at Ohio University before heading to Kraft Foods Microstructure Research Group. His division excelled in creating novel food ingredients, and Martin became an expert in product development and quality assurance. He later moved to Dreyer's Grand Ice Cream, where he developed the company's first analytical laboratory. Oram has a PhD in environmental engineering and spent the last decade researching the decomposition of coastal contaminants, authoring peer-reviewed technical reports, and lecturing extensively at international conferences. In 2009, Martin and Oram started Collective Wellness, which develops protocols for measuring contaminants in cannabis crops.[7] More recently, Martin and Oram were planning to open their own dispensary in the Bay Area city of Martinez.[8]

Another newcomer was former minister Don Morgan, who, after working at several small ministries, became executive director of Bay Respite, a nonprofit that provided in-home care for seniors with severe disabilities. He tripled the size of the organization, which eventually served thousands of families in six Bay Area counties. In 2009, Morgan answered an online job advertisement posted by the ASA. Intrigued by the opportunity to work in a new industry, he signed on as associate director. Morgan said he wasn't looking for a job in the medical marijuana field, and he had no background at all with marijuana. "But I do have experience in healthcare issues, and it seemed very compelling to me. The ASA is the only major advocacy group that works exclusively for patients, and I liked that," Morgan said. "Of course, I spent a lot of time thinking about it and had to convince family and friends that I hadn't lost my mind. I mean, we all grew up with *Reefer Madness* and certain preconceptions about the stoner image."[9]

Several months after taking the job with the ASA, Morgan was hiring for two positions. He noticed that the applicants reflected vastly different backgrounds. "I have been amazed at the diversity, and how overqualified the hundreds of applicants are that want to get into this field now," he said.

After taking a job in the medical marijuana industry in 2005, former corporate manager Dale Clare quickly made her mark by helping reshape the industry's public image. As executive chancellor of Oaksterdam University, Clare traveled all over the state promoting the industry's new professionalism. Besides teaching classes, she lobbied state and local elected officials and helped develop a medical marijuana regulatory council. She was known to teach a morning class in Oakland, drive 90 miles to Sacramento to meet with a legislative aide, return to Oakland for an afternoon class, and then drive 350 miles to teach the next morning at the Los Angeles campus.

Clare is energetic and attractive, with a wavy mop of red hair that sets off both qualities. She said she didn't mind the constant travel because motion was something she was born into. Her mother was a radio and television personality, and her stepfather was the drummer for popular rock band Grand Funk Railroad. As her parents pursued their careers, the family rarely stayed in any one community for more than a year. Clare grew used to constantly changing homes, schools, and friends, and the nomadic lifestyle suited her. When she left home at 18, she simply kept moving. "I was always the new kid in school and then gone again before I could create a niche for myself," Clare said. "And it was okay. I have the restless nature of a gypsy, which is probably why I've always had jobs that require travel. I don't do well in a room unless there's a clear way out of it."[10]

After graduating from the University of Central Florida with a degree in communications, Clare worked in the corporate world for 16 years. She first worked as a territory manager for Alliant Foodservice, Inc., a major corporate food distributor. "They sold over 10,000 line items and ingredients, processed foods, commercial-grade appliances which were distributed to casinos, hospitals, prisons . . . ," Clare said. "You name it—if they sold food, we had our hand in it." From food service, Clare went into research for Proctor & Gamble. She headed a study for Uncle Ben's Rice that determined for the first time that bowl-shaped plastic containers would be popular with frozen food customers. (Clare noted, with a hint of pride, that plastic bowls became the standard in the frozen food industry.) Clare next went to work for global footwear retailer Brown Shoe Company, where she spent six years opening new stores, troubleshooting, and hiring management staff.

But mainstream corporate life wasn't fulfilling for Clare, and she was constantly looking around for something new. "I just felt there had to be something more to life than slinging slop and shoes," she said.

That meaningful career found Clare in 2005. A friend who worked in the cannabis industry offered her a job managing an Orange County medical office that specialized in writing cannabis recommendations. Her initial thought was the office couldn't afford her corporate salary, but she was surprised by a generous offer and accepted the job. Although Clare was not yet a convert to the movement, she slowly became involved in cannabis politics. She started attending NORML meetings and was moved by the injustices of the war on drugs. For the first time in her professional working life, Clare wanted to make social change.

Working in a doctor's office, as it turned out, was not the best place to make that change. She knew her skills and corporate know-how would make her valuable on the industry's front line, so she took a job with the newly formed Oaksterdam University. For Clare, it was a perfect fit. The cannabis industry was in dire need of experienced people who could raise the industry's professional profile. It needed people who could communicate effectively with the public and lawmakers. And, perhaps most importantly, the industry needed people to take leadership roles in bringing together the divergent interests within the industry.

With a convert's zeal, Clare began to help construct a mainstream, corporate-style framework for a quasi-legal industry that was nonconformist by nature. Taxation, legalization of adult use, and regulation were the subjects of sharp disagreements within the ranks of the cannabis industry. Coalitions competed with one another. The patients' coalition wanted access to safe medicine, the growers' coalition wanted a protected market, and the dispensary owners wanted to run their businesses without fear of raids. "What we do is herd cats," Clare said. "At a time when everyone was about to break into different factions and go their separate ways, several organizations emerged to create uniform goals, to unify the individual armies into a coalition that government officials could have confidence in."

The theme of unification ran through all of Clare's work. Her overarching goal was to make the industry credible, professional, and worthy of government and public confidence. If the marijuana industry was going to be taken seriously, new professionals like Clare said it would have to create the same self-regulating institutions that helped govern other industries.

In October 2009, Los Angeles city attorney Carmen Trutanich exploited the lack of medical marijuana testing in an attempt to strike fear in the public. Trutanich claimed a sampling of marijuana confiscated during a police raid on a dispensary was contaminated with a pesticide used to kill Mexican fire ants. In front of a bank of television cameras, he produced a can of Raid bug killer and sprayed the ground with the pesticide. "Now would any of you eat a salad with that sprayed on it?"[11] Trutanich, a regular cigar smoker, did not mention that only a small portion of the confiscated cannabis was tainted with pesticides, or that the American tobacco industry uses about 25 million pounds of pesticides annually on tobacco crops, according to the U.S. General Accounting Office.[12]

Starting in 2007, Clare began to work with other medical marijuana stakeholders like Debbie Goldsberry of the Berkeley Patients Group and Robert Jacob, executive director of Peace in Medicine Healing Center, to form the Medical Cannabis Safety Council. The council aimed to standardize the production and testing of marijuana products and to develop specific business practices for dispensary owners. A dedicated and thorough self-regulatory body like the safety council could make it easier for government officials to publicly support cannabis dispensaries, growing operations, and the industry as a whole. "Health and safety agencies are not concerned with whether cannabis should be legal; they are concerned with whether growers are using reliable equipment," Clare said. "A lot of these things are basic common sense, like keep the dog out of the grow room. But if it's included in a canon of best practices, it puts a face on it that growers and the public can understand."

Clare is also the director of public relations for the Medical Cannabis Association, a trade organization she helped found. The association is in development but will ultimately promote the medical cannabis industry as responsible, safety conscious, and professional. Once up and running, the Medical Cannabis Association will unify industry leaders to set standards for dispensaries, identify political priorities, and provide a unified voice for growers and dispensary owners. "We're trying to model these organizations after the cheese industry," Clare said. "We took a look at what a wonderful job the 'Got Milk' campaign did and thought that's the kind of thing an advisory board can do for the medical cannabis industry."

One of the recurring themes in Oaksterdam University classes is common business courtesy and community outreach. Many workers in the medical cannabis industry were unsure how to interact with the city officials, other businesses, and the public. Sometimes that uncertainty caused them to be shy or avoid contact with people in their communities. That type of behavior, Clare said, can be pernicious. Dispensary owners and their employees should go to city council meetings, join the local chambers of commerce, and support neighborhood beautification projects. "Our fight is to help as many of these folks as possible be part of the solution," Clare said. "Most people will do the right thing if you just tell them how. One of the main things we teach is how to be a good neighbor, because if you don't care about the people on your block, you're going to have a very hard time getting the support of city councils and state assembly members."

In fact, there was overwhelming evidence the cannabis industry was moving forward, one neighborhood a time. One example was West Hollywood, a close-knit, progressive community. In the 1960s, it was a magnet for counterculture youth who flocked to nationally known rock-and-roll clubs like the Whisky A-Go-Go and the Troubadour. In the 1970s, gays were drawn to West Hollywood because of its unincorporated status, which put them out of the reach of the notoriously antigay Los Angeles Police Department. Given its progressive politics, West Hollywood welcomed medical cannabis dispensaries after voters approved Proposition 215. But there was a limit to what the village's residents would tolerate. By 2005, the number of dispensaries had increased dramatically. Residents felt there were too many for the relatively small community of 36,000.

City council members and the Los Angeles County Sheriff's Department began to receive complaints about shady dispensary owners and patients smoking cannabis in plain view. Some of the loudest complaints came from parents and teachers of the Foundation Day School, a private kindergarten and preschool that shared a parking lot with a busy dispensary called the Farmacy. Parents were particularly upset that patients were lighting up in the parking lot. "All of a sudden they started opening up boom, boom, boom, boom, boom," Andrew Rakos, the school's general manager, told the *Los Angeles Times* in 2009. "Our parent organization came to me and said, 'We're not happy about this.' There was an immediate influx of a lot of unsavory people."[13]

Farmacy cofounder JoAnne LaForce had worked as a pharmacist for 30 years. When she became aware of the complaints, she invited teachers and parents to tour her dispensary, banned smoking in the parking lot, and hired security that not only patrolled the dispensary, but also the surrounding area, which was a benefit to the school. LaForce was able to calm the parents, and Rakos became an active supporter of The Farmacy. In 2009, the city notified LaForce that she would have to move her dispensary because it was within 500 feet of the preschool. But Rakos went to the city on The Farmacy's behalf and asked them to make an exception, which was granted. "We felt that it was important for the city to know that there are some businesses that are not only respectful, but listened to the needs of the community," Rakos said.[14]

The medical marijuana industry had come out of the shadows. Dispensary operators regularly attended public meetings and cited the taxes they pay, the number of people they employed, and their contributions to community projects such as Little League teams, housing renovations, park improvements, and streetscape beautification projects. They promoted openness by inviting council members, city administrators, law enforcement officers, and community members to tour their dispensaries. And the message was beginning to permeate the industry's rank and file.

During a lively debate over a proposed medical marijuana ordinance in 2009, several Richmond council members looked confused when dispensary operator John Clay publicly invited the entire council to tour his facility. "I urge you to visit the existing facilities. There isn't an operator here who would deny you access," Clay said. "Meet the people patronizing them, meet the staff. Check it out. You'll find that we're not criminals, we're not dangerous, we're law-abiding citizens who want to do well for our community." Another dispensary operator summed up the industry's new stance to the council. "Please tax us, regulate us. We want to work with you."[15]

And the corporate world wanted to work with the new industry, too. When Mike Aberle returned to his Statewide Insurance office on a cold, gray day in January 2010, he was elated. He had come from a small gathering celebrating the submission of signatures in Sacramento for Richard Lee's Control and Tax 2010 initiative. "It was great to meet with Dale Clare and chat with her face to face," Aberle said. "Submitting those signatures was a very significant moment, and it was great to be part of history."[16]

At first blush, Aberle is not the kind of person one might expect to be an enthusiastic supporter of marijuana's legalization. He came from a Republican family that he described as "Rush Limbaugh" conservative. "My family is very right-wing," Aberle said. "I mean, my mother was a U.S. Marine drill sergeant." Aberle is also a devout Christian. His wife is the worship director at their church, and he is a close friend of his parish's pastor. Aberle was cautious about working with the industry at first. "It's crazy, I suppose, when you think about it, but before I began working on this type of insurance, my pastor and I discussed it," Aberle said. "I also talked about it with my family and nobody had a problem with it. My pastor found nothing wrong with it, so long as it's legal."

Aberle is a good example of how the business side of the cannabis industry was making the transition from a social movement to commercial enterprise. "I believe it's the time, and California is ready for the industry to come out of the dark and become a legitimate enterprise," he said. About three years ago, Aberle introduced the idea of specializing in the medical cannabis industry to his bosses, and he received surprisingly little resistance. In fact, the CEO gave him the name and contact information of a medical cannabis activist he knew. Aberle began researching the industry and steadily gained the support of the larger insurance companies that underwrite his policies. He became one of the first insurance agents in the country to offer policies uniquely designed for the cannabis industry. Dispensary owners can now choose from a range of products designed to protect against theft, spoilage, and equipment breakdown. Aberle also helped develop a policy for commercial real estate owners who leased their property to dispensaries or growers. There was commercial vehicle insurance designed for the transportation and delivery of cannabis. "What we've done," he said, "is taken a standard retail insurance model and taken a little bit of restaurant and deli, mixed them together, and we have a product that specifically meets the needs of dispensary owners."

Aberle had been especially innovative in protecting cannabis crops. In January 2010, he offered a policy for indoor growers, and said outdoor growers would soon have their own policy options. Aberle had been meeting with Oakland city officials to discuss how their planned grow warehouses might be insured. "Regulating large scale grows is where the industry is going, and we've been part of scheduled meetings with city leaders who want to revitalize an industrial area with cannabis-growing operations," Aberle said. "We're working with them to see how we can create insurance for those programs." The one risk Aberle said he was unable to cover was seizure by law enforcement, though even that was on his wish list for the future.

Aberle had embraced the medical marijuana industry. He joined the local chapter of the ASA and regularly attended their meetings, which he said were inspiring. "Hearing from the patients themselves is amazing. It keeps us going," he said. But he was clear that his insurance products would focus on the business wing of the industry, not advocacy. "We are very business minded," he said. "No one has been strictly representing the business side of the industry, and that's who we're fighting for every day. We're developing a resource center where dispensary owners and growers can go for good information about contractors, security guard companies, lawyers, doctors—all free of charge. It will be a central point of information for business people so they will no longer have to go to NORML, MPP, or ASA, which are helpful organizations, but not business-centric."

Aberle said he and Statewide Insurance planned to stay with the cannabis industry for the long term, so he was careful to make sure his clients were as serious as he was. He worked closely with new dispensary owners and growers to make sure they complied with local zoning and planning laws, and if a problem arose during the preliminary inspection of a dispensary, he suggested solutions. He was impressed by his clients' responsiveness. "When you give them a recommendation, they do it," he said. "They are eager to do things the right way." Aberle had turned down applicants because they had inadequate business plans, shady backgrounds, or poor community relations. Statewide had endorsed the industry's best practices, and the company expected its clients to adopt them as well. "We did not get into this just to sell policies. We got into it to build a foundation for the new industry, and our goal is to support it now and tomorrow," Aberle said.

By 2010, Aberle had written 250 policies for the cannabis industry. About half were in California, and the rest were in Montana, New Mexico, and Michigan. He said Colorado had recently become very hot, and that he was receiving more inquiries from Denver than from California. Statewide's underwriting policy in Colorado, where for-profit corporations could own dispensaries, differed from its policies elsewhere. "You start wondering who is behind those dispensaries moneywise. Who is behind the corporate veil?" he said. "Are they people who are actually serious about the industry, or is it somebody that shouldn't be in the business?"

Statewide has played a key role in the cannabis industry's growth. For city officials wondering how to regulate dispensaries or whether to ban them outright, insurance coverage is a stamp of approval. That endorsement could also change the minds of skeptical voters. For Aberle, however, commerce had the upper hand. "It's no longer a movement," Aberle said. "The medical cannabis movement is now a full-fledged business."

The Next Generation

Like any expanding business, the medical cannabis industry had jobs to fill in accounting, management, marketing, public relations, Web design, transportation, research, and other areas. At the same time, it needed to remove the criminal stigma attached to the marijuana trade. One of the best ways to accomplish both goals was to attract a steady stream of young, well-educated people who reflected the industry's new professionalism. The industry managed to do that by working with a popular college-based organization. Just as Wall Street recruited new talent from business schools, the medical cannabis industry worked closely with Students for Sensible Drug Policy (SSDP).

The SSDP's overarching goal is the repeal of all drug laws. Casting the war on drugs as a miserable failure, it wishes to shift drug use out of the criminal justice system and to treat it instead as a public health issue. To that end, the billions of dollars now spent on arresting and incarcerating drug users would be redirected to education and substance abuse programs. The SSDP's goal of decriminalizing all drugs doesn't jibe perfectly with the medical marijuana industry's laserlike focus on making cannabis legal, but the student organization shares enough objectives with the industry to make them a near-perfect match. The industry can tap a source of educated, fresh-faced young employees dedicated to social change, and students can work in an industry that encourages their activism and offers well-paying jobs.

Founded in 1998 with five chapters, the SSDP now has more than 200 chapters in the United States, the United Kingdom, Canada, Australia, and Nigeria. The SSDP headquarters in San Francisco was receiving up to five new chapter requests every day. That growth has garnered the SSDP influence on campuses and has attracted the attention of prominent elected officials. "We see ourselves primarily as advocates, and one of our primary goals is to recruit the next generation of activists," said SSDP executive director Micah Daigle.[17]

The SSDP saw a surge in membership after Barack Obama's election in 2008, and students who believe drugs should be decriminalized were encouraged by Obama's decision to appoint R. Gil Kerlikowske as director of National Drug Control Policy. As police chief of Seattle, Kerlikowske was well known for his progressive approach to enforcing marijuana laws. He invited the group to participate in his office's discussions of a new national strategy for controlling drugs. "What he said when he asked us to participate in this process was 'You represent the mainstream now. You represent the majority of Americans who say the war on drugs has been a failure,'" Daigle said. "All the signs are pointing toward reform, and students see it as inevitable. The times are a-changin', and college students want to be part of that."

The SSDP is active on a variety of levels. On campus, its members work to change drug policies, such as unannounced dormitory searches or mandatory eviction for possession of small amounts of drugs. They also lobby university administrations to enact Good Samaritan policies that protect students from punishment if they call authorities to report drug or alcohol emergencies, such as overdoses. One of the SSDP's primary issues was repealing a provision of the Higher Education Act that excluded students with drug convictions from receiving federal financial aid. Since the passage of the act in 1998, the provision prevented more than 200,000 students from applying for federal financial aid even though most had been convicted of misdemeanor offenses such as possession. Largely through SSDP's leadership, Congress altered the provision in 2009 so that only students with felony convictions would be ineligible for aid.

At the state level, the SSDP has advocated for a lower drinking age on the grounds that if teenage alcohol consumption were legal, it would occur in safer environments that were also less conducive to binge drinking. In 2009, the organization helped change drug policies on more than a dozen college campuses. In Rhode Island, the SSDP worked to establish the state's medical cannabis law in 2006; three years later, the Brown University chapter helped develop a state law that allows the distribution of medical cannabis through dispensaries.[18] The SSDP has also addressed drug-related incidents involving students.[19]

A former chapter leader at the University of Rhode Island, Daigle organized a coalition of 20 student organizations against punitive campus drug policies. Their protest at the university president's office received national media attention and led to a policy change that required campus authorities to use discretion when contacting police about students with small amounts of cannabis.

It would be a mistake to assume that the SSDP is composed

primarily of stoners. In fact, its members try to project a more professional image. The organization's Web site shows dozens of young people with open faces and bright smiles, some wearing business suits. "We have many members who have never smoked a joint in their lives," Daigle said. The SSDP is in many ways a reflection of a new national attitude toward drugs in general and cannabis in particular. Since the 1950s, students have been more open-minded about drugs than society as a whole, and that trait is perhaps even more evident in the current generation. The children of baby boomers, they were less likely to hear Anslinger-styled falsehoods and hysterical misconceptions from their parents. According to Daigle, some students join because a substance abuse problem landed a relative in prison instead of rehab. Others are motivated by social justice issues, such as racial disparities in drug convictions and prison sentences.

Daigle said his own reasons for joining the SSDP were typical of most members. "I don't know any students that didn't get involved because of an emotional hook. Everyone has some sort of personal story: someone they know who had trouble with drug addiction or a similar story of hardship related to drugs. A story that is meaningful to them," he said. "Something that makes them aware of the other."

When Daigle was an 18-year-old design major at the University of Rhode Island, he was an introvert who spent most of his free time drawing in his dorm room. But shortly after joining SSDP, he began to develop an acute social awareness. He attended an SSDP conference where he met Jim Miller, the husband of Cheryl Miller, the medical cannabis activist and patient who suffered from severe multiple sclerosis. Despite her severe disability, Miller made numerous trips from her New Jersey home to Washington,

DC, where she lobbied on behalf of the States Rights to Medical Cannabis Act. In 1998, Miller received national attention when she was arrested for smoking cannabis outside of the office of Rep. James Rogan, who had recanted his support of the legislation.

Daigle also met Clifford Thornton, a retired African-American telephone company executive and Green Party candidate for governor in Connecticut. Thornton had been staunchly antidrug after his mother died from a heroin overdose when he was a high school senior. But Thornton had come to believe it was the unregulated black market that had killed his mother, and he became an outspoken advocate for changing drug laws and particularly ending cannabis prohibition.[20] "After that conference, I realized how many people are affected by drug prohibition," Daigle said. "I realized the legalization is about more than just myself, and a transformation began."

Daigle, a self-described responsible pot smoker at that time, became more serious about his activism. By the time he was 20, he was skipping the tie-dyed shirts and Phish concerts and wearing conservative clothing and close-cropped hair. "I didn't feel like I could be stoned all day and be effective at changing the world," Daigle said. "And I thought I wouldn't be taken seriously if I looked like I just came from a Grateful Dead concert."

Daigle lost much of his shyness and became popular enough to be elected to the University of Rhode Island's student senate. He redoubled his volunteer work at the SSDP by helping to organize events and using his design skills to craft flyers announcing them. He wrote for the school newspaper and suddenly found himself being interviewed by newspapers like the *Christian Science Monitor*. Daigle also experienced what he described as "clarity" about politics. "I had a very cynical view of activism before the SSDP because I thought activism was about waving signs and shouting at The Man. I thought it was about burning bridges," Daigle said. "Those things have their place, but I learned it's the other way around, it's about relationship building, finding common ground. I learned that we all have more common ground than not."

After graduating in 2006, Daigle began working full time as the SSDP executive director and has been a critical link between the SSDP and the California medical cannabis industry. "I'm a very different person because of the SSDP," Daigle said. "When the medical cannabis industry hires one of our alumni, that's what they are getting, people who have developed effective political skills who are very serious and are committed to making a difference."

The SSDP had been strongest on the East Coast, and Daigle was charged with raising the organization's West Coast presence. He opened an office in San Francisco, developed ties with the cannabis industry, involved the organization in regional political activity, and began tapping into West Coast funding opportunities.

At a 2009 SSDP fundraiser in San Francisco, the Bay Area medical cannabis industry came out to show its support and establish ties with the student group. Those in attendance included Steve DeAngelo, executive director of Oakland's Harborside Health Center, Michael Nolin of San Francisco's Green Door, Aundre Speciale, codirector of Sacramento's Capitol Wellness Collective, and F. Aaron Smith, the California policy director for the Marijuana Policy Project (MPP). The event was held in a spacious, well-decorated loft and featured an impressive buffet and open bar. The host was both entertaining and informative. A professionally prepared video concisely listed the group's recent accomplishments and laid out its goals. The event raised more than $20,000 for the SSDP.

In the San Francisco Bay Area, SSDP members have been hired by politically active dispensaries such as the Berkeley Patients Group, Harborside, and the Revolutionary Love Project. "Folks in the cannabis industry, when looking for employees, they don't necessarily look for the basic cannabis enthusiast but people who want to make a difference, people who really care about contributing to the advancement of medical marijuana," Daigle said.

The SSDP's activist bent was prominent at the organization's 11th annual conference in 2010. Becky DeKeuster, the Berkeley Patients Group's community liaison, opened the weekend-long event with a rousing speech to 300 students in a large hall in San Francisco. She concluded her talk by inviting the students to tour her dispensary and to learn more about its tradition of political activism. The Berkeley Patients Group and Oakland's Harborside Health Center also rented booths at the conference for recruitment. It was the first time the SSDP's annual convention had a job fair component. "The SSDP does a great job of turning out people who are passionate about making change and fearless about educating people," DeKeuster said. "And for us, that's what activism is really all about—teaching people."

Another speaker was Ethan Nadelmann, executive director of the Drug Policy Alliance, who discussed the rising popularity of legalizing marijuana for adult use. He ran down the Gallup Poll numbers, which showed a huge jump in support for legalization. Nationwide, 44 percent of voters support legalization; of those under 50 fully half did so; and in the western states, the figure was 54 percent. He reminded the students that they should not get too caught up in making money, but instead should focus on the movement for social justice. "I want you to remember that as marijuana becomes institutionalized and all these jobs are opening up, it's still a movement, and there's a long way to go," Nadelmann told the cheering crowd. "So once you graduate and go work for Harborside, remember that. I hope many of you go out there and become rich, but once you do, make sure you remember us."[21]

CHAPTER 7

The New Politicians

Bundled against the midwinter chill, hundreds of people formed a line outside a warehouse in the bleak industrial district that sprawls between Interstate 80 and the Oakland Airport. They were waiting for the grand opening of iGrow, a 15,000-square-foot megastore that was promoting itself as "The Walmart of Weed." The store offered anything you might need to cultivate cannabis. Displayed on the 15-foot-tall aisle racks were expensive lighting and ventilation systems, state-of-the-art hydroponics, and a wide selection of nutrients with catchy names like "Bud Factor." In the style of a Home Depot, the store had helpful staff members, each wearing a black polo shirt with the store's logo emblazoned on it. The store also offered cultivation classes, grow-room construction advice, and even a "doc in the box"—an onsite doctor who could write a recommendation on the spot, which would allow Oakland residents to grow up to 72 plants in their homes.

There was an air of excitement among those waiting in line. They were mostly male, though there were some parents who held the hands of small children while they waited patiently for the opening. On the other side of a six-foot metal fence that surrounded the iGrow parking lot, a bank of local and national television news cameras, newspaper reporters, and city dignitaries were waiting for the ribbon-cutting ceremony to begin.

The gates opened, and the line of customers swarmed into the parking lot and formed a semicircle around the front door. Oakland Councilwoman Rebecca Kaplan walked into the glare of the camera lights and, surrounded by two other city council members, made a short but exuberant speech about the new jobs and city revenue the superstore would generate. "The grow business is an economic opportunity for our city," Kaplan said. "We want to celebrate, we want to support, and we want to uplift that to help pay for the parks, libraries, and services that people need."

Progressive politicians have a long history of supporting the marijuana social movement as it struggled against tough laws and a hostile public. Local politicians like San Francisco's George Moscone, Harvey Milk, Terence Hallinan, Tom Ammiano, and Mark Leno and Oakland's Nate Miley and Nancy Nadel were instrumental in creating a protective canopy that allowed the medical cannabis movement to take hold. But now that the movement is quickly transitioning into an industry, it requires another type of politician—one who can ensure that cannabis becomes an accepted part of the community's economy and government. Kaplan is perhaps the best example of the new progressive who is working closely with the industry as it transitions into a vital economic feature of local communities.

Some politicians who are openly supportive of the medical marijuana industry by promoting regulations and taxation find themselves in tricky situations. The new industry has been forged largely at the local level by county supervisors and city council members who have tinkered with various regulatory models until they found one that fit their community. Oftentimes, when a progressive politician promotes regulations that are intended to help legitimize the industry, medical marijuana advocates, patients, and dispensary owners can be hostile.

In 2005, while progressive San Francisco supervisor Ross Mirkarimi was working on the city's new medical marijuana ordinance, he found himself having to explain to his upset liberal supporters that there were too many dispensaries in the city and neighbors were starting to complain. Furthermore, the larger dispensaries were gaining unfair influence in the absence of regulations. "There's 'Big Pot' now; there is a monopoly interest in clubs who want to have a corner on the market," Mirkarimi said.[1]

In Oakland, Kaplan embraced the role of new progressive with gusto. Her career has risen in part on the tide of medical marijuana's surging popularity. The 38-year-old Kaplan made a bold political debut in 2008. An openly gay attorney, she ran for the city's only at-large council seat, and her outspoken support for the city's medical marijuana dispensaries seemed to be an asset. She won endorsements from probusiness interests, such as developers and the Oakland Metropolitan Chamber of Commerce, and was popular with the city's growing artist community, activists, and labor unions. Her opponent was Kerry Hamill, the 52-year-old former chief of staff to Don Perata, an influential member of California's powerful Democratic political machine. Perata steered endorsements and campaign contributions to Hamill, but Kaplan won with a stunning 62 percent of the vote. Since then, she has been at the forefront of regulating Oakland's dispensaries and helped write the first ordinance in the state to levy a special tax on dispensary profits.

Oakland politics was ready for new blood. Older politicians

with illustrious careers in state and federal politics, most notably Ron Dellums and Jerry Brown, had controlled the mayor's office for years. Dellums's tenure was especially controversial, largely due to the perception that he was an absentee mayor. Kaplan, on the other hand seemed to be all over town, and she was quite obviously connected tightly to the medical cannabis industry. She received significant contributions from the industry, and many of her highly motivated campaign volunteers were Oaksterdam University students or dispensary employees. In fact, her former campaign office was converted into the school's student union.

Although Kaplan's industry connections clearly benefited her campaign, she said she would have been equally outspoken about her support if they had been a political liability. "I think there have been a lot of politicians who avoid talking about pot because they worry that everybody will get freaked out," Kaplan said. "It's the same thing with gay rights. It wasn't that long ago that if you stood up for gay rights, you would be mocked and derided."[2]

She pointed out that she is not just a pot politician. She has supported transit-oriented development, public safety issues, and economic development. Nonetheless, as a candidate, Kaplan had cannabis credibility. Ever since Kaplan had studied law, she had staunchly opposed the prohibition of marijuana. As a member of the Alameda County transportation board, she was active in the successful 2004 campaign for Oakland's Measure Z, which made Oakland the first city to openly regulate medical marijuana dispensaries. She was less interested in medical cannabis than in the government hypocrisy that characterized marijuana prohibition. "I wasn't driven by the pot; I was driven by the lack of integrity in government," she said.

Kaplan was particularly offended by President Richard Nixon's dismissal of a 1972 report compiled by the National Commission on Marijuana and Drug Abuse, also known as the Shafer Commission. Nixon formed the commission to study marijuana and determine whether it was dangerous. Nixon wanted the study to dovetail with the Controlled Substances Act, which another committee was drafting. Nixon stacked the 13-member Shafer Commission with 9 conservative Republicans, hoping to steer its findings against marijuana. But when committee chairman Governor Raymond Shafer presented the report to Congress in 1972, Nixon was profoundly disappointed. The commission found no connection between the use of cannabis and crime. It further determined it was impossible to die from a cannabis overdose and found no evidence marijuana use led to addiction or psychosis. The report concluded that the "actual and potential harm of use of the drug is not great enough to justify intrusion by the criminal law into private behavior, a step which our society takes only with the greatest reluctance."[3] Nixon ignored the study and continued to support strict laws against marijuana. When he created the Drug Enforcement Administration by executive order in 1973, he insisted marijuana be given high priority. By 1979, the DEA had begun its Marijuana Eradication Program, which has resulted in an ongoing war on marijuana users, growers, and sellers.

For Kaplan, Nixon's treatment of the Shafer Commission's findings was one of the greatest government injustices in American history. "I was only two years old when the Shafer Report came out, but I can see the result of Nixon's ignoring it. You have millions of people in prison, huge racial disparities, huge social costs, and it's all based on lies," she said. "Another thing that is amazing is the cult of silence that surrounds the hypocrisy. Everybody in government knew the war on marijuana was unwarranted, but they kept silent while millions of lives were destroyed and families ruined. It's an outrageous example of an unethical and destructive government act."

Once elected, Kaplan began work with the Oakland dispensaries to write Measure F, the first U.S. ordinance to allow a special local taxation of cannabis sales. The landmark measure's popularity sent a highly charged signal to cash-strapped cities throughout California. Kaplan's office—as well as other city offices and medical marijuana organizations—was flooded with calls from local officials who wanted to use Measure F as a model for their cities. In 2004, Oakland also blazed new ground with Measure Z, which was the first local ordinance to regulate dispensaries. "At that time, no cities had permitting ordinances in place because they were afraid of federal prosecution," Kaplan said. "Cities were afraid of the feds punishing them, and the other thing was that there would be a dispensary paper trail that would give the DEA a lead in raiding and prosecuting them."

The medical cannabis industry now had the support of Oakland council members, law enforcement, business organizations, and the public. Because of that success, Kaplan wanted to cautiously raise the current limit from four dispensaries to seven or eight. "Demand is very high, but I think it's best to move very slowly, despite some of our allies in the movement who think there should be no numerical limits on dispensaries," Kaplan said. "It's good to go slow because to the extent you can control them and show they work well, it's good for the city, good for the patients, and good for the industry as a whole."

Kaplan was working on complex legislation to make Oakland the first city to oversee large-scale indoor cannabis farms. The Goldman School of Public Policy at the University of California, Berkeley, was working with Kaplan's office on some of the trickier details, such as how to protect city employees from arrest should they be in possession of marijuana samples. The city would issue licenses to farmers and then monitor their practices and test their harvests to ensure the cannabis was free of contaminants, fertilizers, mold, or mildew. One study commissioned by a developer in 2010 found that a proposal to build a 172,000-square-foot growing facility on a 7.4-acre site could generate $2 million in new revenues and create as many as 350 union jobs.

"There have been problems with grow operations: there's fire danger from jury-rigged wiring, unlicensed property alterations to accommodate grow rooms, and there have been robberies. We can do for growing what we did for dispensaries," Kaplan said. "With regulations, we can do fire safety and background checks, require security guards, make sure they are in industrial areas away from residential neighborhoods and schools. And it would mean a lot of jobs. We have a lot of vacant warehouses in Oakland."

Several months after the interview, Kaplan proposed first-of-its-kind legislation that would allow Oakland to offer permits to as many as four large-scale growers.

Since Kaplan's election, her popularity has continued to grow, and she said she was considering a run for mayor in 2010, which her supporters encouraged. One competitor would be 64-year-old Don Perata, who was termed out of his state senator's seat in 2008. A formidable and well-connected politician, Perata will certainly have access to more money as well as a pocket full of chits for political endorsements. The only question is whether Oakland voters want a mayor that can, for a change, reflect the city's new vitality. For Kaplan, the cannabis industry has a significant role in the city's future. "There's a lot happening here. The theater dis-

trict is doing well, and we have a growing art scene and a great
nightlife with places like the Uptown. . . . There's the alternative
foodie, herbivore restaurant thing taking off, and the cannabis
industry is part of all that," Kaplan said. "There's a lot of exciting
things happening here, and the job of being Oakland's mayor ain't
a retirement job."

The Marijuana Lobby

For local officials unfamiliar with the marijuana industry, there
was a new breed of consultant available to help hammer out regulations and successful policies. Although political consultants and
lobbyists have been working for nonprofit advocacy groups like
NORML or the Marijuana Policy Alliance for years, they were
starting to represent medical marijuana business interests for the
first time. Perhaps that development led *Esquire* magazine to put
"marijuana lobbyist" on its list of 10 New Jobs for Men in 2010.[4]

Max Del Real was one such consultant. Sitting at a café on
Berkeley's trendy Fourth Street in early 2010, Del Real checked his
Blackberry while talking earnestly about the burgeoning cannabis
industry. With his business suit and his thick black hair combed
neatly back, he bore a resemblance to 1950s movie star Victor
Mature. Del Real is gregarious and he can suddenly break into a
parody of the stereotypical bonhomous lobbyist. ("Yeah, I went
to UC Berkeley. I met my wife there. She was a triathlete, and I
was drunk . . . it happens.")

Del Real immediately distinguished himself from the medical
marijuana movement. "I am not a patient advocate. I have complete and total respect for the patients' rights advocates and what
they have achieved, but I am at the forefront of a new industry,"

he said. "As a movement and an industry, we need to get into business suits and look more like capitalists than cannabis advocates."

A former high school teacher, Del Real now runs his own lobbying firm, California Capitol Solutions, but he had also served as the legislative director of BOSS Enterprises, a medical-marijuana consulting firm with a stronger background in business than political activism. Michael Nolin, who founded BOSS in 2009, was the owner of the Green Door dispensary in San Francisco. Nolin started BOSS Enterprises because he saw a need for dispensary owners, medical-cannabis entrepreneurs, and government officials to find pragmatic solutions to emerging problems in the industry. BOSS's vice president, Nathan McPhail, was a practicing attorney with a background in investment banking. He spent many years at Merrill Lynch, where he worked on an investment team that managed more than $400 million in assets, according to the BOSS Web site. BOSS helped city officials and entrepreneurs navigate the mined labyrinth of conflicting state laws, community sensibilities, and potential political blowback. It also offered advice on the testing of cannabis for impurities and counseled prospective investors.

Another consulting firm, CannBe, was formed in 2009. Formerly Harborside Management Associates (HMA), CannBe focused on the medical cannabis patient. Its principals included Steve DeAngelo, the owner of the celebrated Harborside Health Center, and ASA's California director Don Duncan. CannBe's principals also included Robert Jacob, the owner of Peace In Medicine, a holistic dispensary in Sebastopol, California; and James Anthony, a land-use attorney who helped write Oakland's Measure F and cofounded the Cannabis Collective, which sought to create access to medical marijuana to low-income patients. According to CannBe's Web site, the firm "brings the most experienced and accomplished professionals in the medical cannabis industry together under one roof—the A-Team of medical cannabis. With unmatched records of individual success, the CannBe team offers a unique capacity to develop, launch, and direct medical cannabis projects—from concept to reality."[5]

Based in Sacramento, Del Real has a strong knowledge of government processes as well as good working relationships with many state legislators, county supervisors, and council members. He lives with his wife and two children just north of Sacramento and spends a great deal of time on the road, with frequent trips to the Bay Area as well as other towns and counties around the state. Although he often ends his statements on a note of levity, Del Real is serious when it comes to the cannabis industry. His consulting business has increased since Attorney General Eric Holder announced the Department of Justice would no longer prosecute dispensaries, cultivators, or patients who are in compliance with state law. "There has been a dispensary boom in cities and towns around the state. In Sacramento, there has been an increase in dispensaries of 200 percent since Holder's announcement," he said. "Right now, we're working in five different counties, talking to planning departments, city managers, chiefs of police, and community organizations. We essentially guide them—help them open quality dispensaries that will be a benefit to the community and city."

Entrepreneurs frequently opened dispensaries in towns without medical cannabis ordinances. The owners' hope was that once the city approved an ordinance, the dispensary would be grandfathered in. Del Real advised against that practice because it was disrespectful to government process. "If you're going to be successful, you have to start on common ground. You have to have a working relationship with the city."

Each city preferred to tailor its ordinance to local needs and pressures, and according to Del Real, that meant reinventing the wheel each time he worked with new government officials. He looked forward to comprehensive state legislation. "We're trying to move beyond that, and I'm convinced this is the year of cannabis," he said with characteristic enthusiasm. "We have Tom Ammiano backing a bill in Sacramento, we have Supervisor David Campos expanding the cannabis industry in San Francisco, and Councilmember Rebecca Kaplan leading that city to the state's first city-controlled grow warehouse. The rest of the state—the rest of the country—is watching these efforts." According to Del Real, such comprehensive state legislation would soon put the medical cannabis industry on par with any other industry.

Industry advocates had already forged relationships with key legislators, such as state assemblyman Tom Ammiano. In fact, tickets for a recent fundraiser attended exclusively by the cannabis industry started at $250 and ran to $2,500. BOSS also anticipated safety standards and testing of cannabis, and they have partnered with Collective Wellness Inc., a group of research scientists who have backgrounds in standardized testing for food products. "Collective Wellness has a three-person staff that includes two PhDs, and what they bring to the table is decades of experience in scientific food testing," Del Real said. "These guys are real scientists. Now I'm a scientist of communications, which means I buy the drinks."

Along with BOSS and CannBe, Del Real's firm was designed to find the mutual benefits between business and government. He predicted the next phase of legitimacy for the industry was government-regulated growing operations. He was working with elected officials, insurance agents, longtime cannabis cultivators, and other corporate interests as they tried to set up city-sanctioned grow warehouses in Oakland, San Francisco, Los Angeles, and Sacramento. "City-managed grows are the next big thing," Del Real said, "and they will bring corporate America in as partners— as insurers first. Who knows what's next?" According to Del Real, "There is a beautiful opportunity before all of us, and I can tell you that cities are no longer shy about asking how they can make money on this. They need money, and they want to know how to regulate and tax the industry."

Del Real was convinced that legalization of the adult use of cannabis was at hand, and it would be a game changer for the industry. The medical fig leaf would be removed, and the not-for-profit requirement under Proposition 215 would no longer be in place. Corporations and limited partnerships would be able to participate in the cannabis business for the first time. And that meant large investments in dispensaries, grow operations, edible goods, and all the attendant businesses that dovetail with the cannabis industry. "Right now, if you're sitting on a big pile of money in New York and you want to invest in the California cannabis industry, there's nowhere you can go," Del Real said. "You can't go to your stockbroker, but you can go to California Capitol Solutions."

Del Real's Blackberry had been going off throughout the interview, and he announced that he was late for his next appointment. Before he hurried off, he mentioned that several documentary filmmakers had asked him to put them in touch with the industry's key people. "It's just another indication of how hot things are for the cannabis industry," he said as he stood up. His face broke into a broad smile as he reached out for a hearty handshake. "Things are on fire, but it's okay because we're the firemen."

Del Real may be right about legalization. If California's Regulate, Control, and Tax Cannabis 2010 ballot initiative succeeds, it will drastically change the industry in California and across the country. But the initiative has been even more controversial within the medical cannabis industry than outside of it.

CHAPTER 8

Legalization

In 1911, after years of scandal and high-profile corruption trials, California voters overwhelmingly approved one of the most open ballot initiative laws in the country. The idea was to allow voters to bypass state lawmakers when they were too timid, cowed, or corrupt to act on the voters' behalf. Almost a century later, the process is still relatively simple and accessible. Any group or individual can write an initiative and submit it with a $200 fee to the state attorney general's office. After the initiative's fiscal cost was analyzed, the signature gathering began. If the authors didn't have access to a large group of well-organized volunteers, signature gatherers could be easily hired at a price. For about $1 million, a professional company would send paid staffers to shopping malls, commercial districts, and public transportation hubs to collect the roughly 440,000 signatures of registered voters required to qualify the initiative for the California ballot. And if the initiative won 50 percent of the vote on Election Day, it became law.

That form of direct democracy has given California voters a powerful tool to shape their state and influence others. For example, Californians ignited a nationwide movement toward property tax relief with the passage of Proposition 13 in 1978. Citizens have bypassed the state legislature to make laws on tobacco tax, term limits, casinos, wildlife protection, gay marriage, and, of course, medical marijuana.

Oaksterdam University founder and dispensary owner Richard Lee took the lead on legalization in 2009. He coauthored the legislation and put up more than $800,000 of his own money to collect the qualifying signatures. Lee's initiative was aimed at swing voters—those who supported medical cannabis, for example, but might not want a dispensary in their neighborhood. If approved, the Regulate, Control, and Tax Cannabis Act of 2010 would allow anyone 21 or older to possess or transport up to an ounce of cannabis. It would allow the taxation of the cultivation and retail sales of cannabis. Any store that so chose could sell individual customers up to an ounce, and it would be legal to cultivate as much cannabis as you could grow in a 25-foot-square area.

The initiative would also create new laws regarding marijuana use. It would be illegal to smoke marijuana in public or in the presence of a minor. Cities and counties could ban the sale of cannabis, though not its possession. And existing prohibitions against the operation of vehicles, boats, and aircraft while under the influence of marijuana would remain in place. The new law would not replace Proposition 215. Patients could still possess or cultivate marijuana according to local limits. In Oakland, for example, a patient could grow 72 plants indoors, but nonpatients would be restricted to what they could fit in a five-by-five area, or roughly 24 plants.

With the public's growing acceptance of cannabis, Lee decided 2010 was as good an election year as any to back the first state legalization effort in California since the 1970s. "We see a lot of things making it right for this time," Lee said. "The budget crisis here in California, the violence in Mexico, the economy continuing to decline, the polls—all suggest that this may be the time to do it." He may be right. Masterson & Wright, the company that Lee hired to collect signatures, racked up more than 700,000—39 percent more than the required minimum. Proponents set a goal of raising $10 million for the campaign, about five times more than opponents were expecting to spend.[1]

Endorsements came rolling in, some from unexpected quarters. Randi Weingarten, president of the 850,000-member American Federation of Teachers, and retired Seattle police chief Norm Stamper endorsed the measure. Retired Los Angeles sheriff's deputy Jeffrey Studdard was the spokesperson for a statewide radio campaign. Former superior court judge James P. Gray supported the effort. "As a retired Orange County judge, I've been on the front lines of the drug war for three decades, and I know from experience that the current approach is simply not working," Gray said. "Controlling marijuana with regulations similar to those currently in place for alcohol will put street drug dealers and organized crime out of business."

The California NAACP supported the initiative because of the huge racial disparity in arrests. "In California, African Americans make up 7 percent of the population, but 22 percent of the marijuana arrests," said state president Alice Huffman. "I see it as a civil rights issue because so many of our young people get their start in the criminal justice system over a joint."[2] Several labor unions were also considering endorsing the initiative. The United Food and Commercial Workers International Union, which unionized the first cannabis workers in the United States, was particularly interested. "I believe it will create tens of thousands of sustainable, single-earner union jobs in the long run," said union member Dan Rush. "All the way from the agricultural process to the retail process to the food processing process to the transportation process."[3]

In another sign that the cannabis industry was taking on a corporate mentality, Lee hired campaign consultant Chris Lehane as a strategist. Lehane had worked for mainstream Democrats like Bill Clinton, John Kerry, and Gray Davis, but he had also taken on more controversial clients. In 2007, when the Writers Guild of America struck the large studios, Lehane and his partner, Mark Fabiani, represented the Alliance of Motion Picture and Television Producers, which includes major entertainment corporations such as CBS, NBC, and Sony Pictures. By squaring off against the union, Lehane and Fabiani earned the scorn of Andy Stern, the powerful head of the 1.9-million-member Service Employees International Union (SEIU). During the strike, Stern announced that the SEIU and the Change to Win Federation of labor unions were severing all ties with Lehane's company.

But there was opposition in the industry. Prominent dispensary owners, cannabis attorneys, and nonprofit advocacy groups were reluctant to endorse the initiative. They criticized the way it was written, and some pressured Lee to hold off until 2012, when more voters, especially younger ones, would turn out to vote for president. Ultimately, however, the industry cautiously rallied around the initiative. The three major nonprofits that advocate for legalization of cannabis were the first to come around. They were primarily concerned about the timing, but once the petitions were certified, they threw in their full support.

The California initiative shifted attention away from lobbying efforts in Washington. The Marijuana Policy Project (MPP), based in Washington, DC, focuses its lobbying efforts in the Beltway, and its political action committee has contributed to numerous federal elections. But Aaron Houston, MPP's chief lobbyist, said the energy for legalization is occurring at the state level. "We are becoming more decentralized," he said. "The sheer volume of supporters dictates that a top-down strategy would not work at this point. Decentralization is a critical component to tactical success."[4]

Drug Policy Alliance executive director Ethan Nadelmann was also a staunch supporter of the California initiative. "Now it's time again for California to lead the way in ending the follies of marijuana prohibition in favor of a responsible policy of tax and regulation," he said.[5]

NORML executive director Alan St. Pierre said his organization was solidly behind the initiative. "We'll launch a major effort in which we'll try to redirect every dollar out there to California to help with the legalization effort this year," St. Pierre vowed.[6]

Internal Dissent

But there was still strong resistance to Lee's initiative, and much of it was coming from his allies. One of the earliest critics was Steve DeAngelo, the high-profile CEO of Oakland's Harborside Health Center dispensary, which has been featured in dozens of national television, radio, and print stories. With its upscale, banklike interior, Harborside had been held up as a model for community orientation, professionalism, and its work with local governments. It claimed to have the widest selection of cannabis strains and was at the forefront of testing products for contaminants.

DeAngelo has touted his history as a cannabis activist. He helped organize the Proposition 59 campaign in 1998, which legalized medical cannabis in Washington, DC, and he is a cofounder and charter member of the ASA. And despite his long braids, trademark fedora, and latter-day-hippie appearance, DeAngelo is an astute businessman. In 1991, he founded Ecolution, which sells hemp products to retail stores throughout the United States and in 21 other countries. In 2006, he opened Harborside, which he claims has 48,000 members and serves roughly 800 people a day. Offering its members free appointments with an onsite neuropath, acupuncturist, and chiropractor, Harborside grosses about $20 million a year. The dispensary pays $2 million annually in state sales tax and another $360,000 for Oakland's local dispensary levy.[7] DeAngelo and his partner, Dave Wedding Dress, expanded their dispensary operation to San Jose in 2010.

DeAngelo was initially outspoken in his opposition to Lee's legalization initiative. At the 2009 NORML convention in San Francisco, he denounced the legalization effort as a reckless flirtation that could severely damage the entire medical cannabis industry. After speaking with neighbors, police, and city officials, DeAngelo said he concluded they were opposed to legalization. "Their discomfort springs from the lack of any positive image of what legal cannabis distribution would look like," he said. Californians envisioned "armed dealers setting up shop and slinging weed on corners of their suburban neighborhoods." They feared their children would be brainwashed by "glossy ads for reefer in the style of Anheuser-Busch."[8]

To support his position, DeAngelo quoted a *Fortune* magazine article in which writer Roger Parloff advocated a slow approach to legalization. Parloff argued the entire cannabis industry was at risk if California's dispensaries failed. "If [proponents] succeed, they'll convince the fence sitter and lead the way to a nationwide metamorphosis. If they fail, the backlash will be savage," DeAngelo read from the article. "If communities cannot adequately regulate the dispensaries, they'll descend into unsightly, youth-seducing, crime-ridden playgrounds for gang-bangers, and this flirtation with legalization will conclude the way the last one did: with a swift and merciless swing of the pendulum."[9]

Although most California communities have been managing dispensaries without such hellish consequences, DeAngelo told the gathering that Parloff's speculations were valid. "As one of those with his head on the chopping block, I am very concerned about that pendulum," he said. "We must embrace the not-for-profit, community-service model of cannabis distribution. When you boil down the fear of our 25 percent of swing voters, I would submit that it likely comes down to them not wanting us as a society to make the same mistakes with cannabis that we made with alcohol and tobacco: glamorization, excessive advertising driving inappropriate use, profit-making corporations enticing their children into lifetimes of dependency."

Instead, DeAngelo recommended waiting five to six years while the medical cannabis industry took hold in more states and established a solid track record. "Across the nation, thousands of not-for-profit community-service dispensaries have created a positive model of cannabis distribution," he told his audience. He also suggested the legalization would occur organically. "At dispensaries all across the country, we will stop asking for medical cannabis identification and simply ask for adult identification. We will flip the switch at the dispensary door, and all adult Americans will have what hundreds of thousands of Californians now have—free, safe, and affordable access to cannabis."[10] But once the California attorney general qualified the initiative for the 2010 state ballot, DeAngelo reluctantly offered his support to the campaign and even promised to contribute $1,000 to the effort.[11]

Other allies were also grumbling openly about the initiative. One was attorney Robert Raich, legal counsel to California's earliest dispensary owners. Raich's credentials are extensive. He has lectured widely on the regulation of medical cannabis and was a member of the California attorney general's Medical Marijuana Task Force, which crafted much of the language for SB 420. He also worked on the only two medical cannabis cases argued before the Supreme Court: *United States v. Oakland Cannabis Buyers' Cooperative* in 2001 and *Gonzalez v. Raich* (no relation) in 2005. In addition, Raich had taught medical cannabis awareness classes to Oakland Police Department cadets.

Although Raich taught at Oaksterdam University, he disagreed with Richard Lee when it came to Control and Tax 2010. Raich was wary of the new restrictions the initiative would create, such as prohibiting use in front of minors or in public places, outlawing sales to anyone between the ages of 18 and 20, and restricting growing space to 25 square feet, which Raich said was ridiculously inadequate.

Raich asked Lee to make changes to the initiative, but he refused. Raich suspected campaign consultants had given Lee poor advice and convinced him he needed to curry the votes of soccer moms, who theoretically feel more comfortable voting for tight restrictions. "In fact, when I look through the eyes of someone who is unfamiliar with cannabis, I see so many restrictions that we might actually lose votes. The voter is going to say, 'This guy is a proponent who knows more about weed than anybody, and he wants so many restrictions that it must really be a dangerous drug.'"[12]

Raich said that it was foolish to make so many concessions to a perceived public resistance to legalization, that voters are typically driven by emotion rather than logic, and that most people don't read the ballot text of a new law in detail. "This initiative will be decided based on two words, 'legalize' and 'marijuana,' yes or no? That's all people really care about, all they'll know about, all they want to know about."

Often called the spiritual father of the medical marijuana movement, Dennis Peron coauthored Proposition 215. He said Lee's initiative was so restrictive it was nothing less than a declaration of war. Peron has always favored a community-based vision of medical marijuana in which the drug was dispensed at affordable prices with as little commerce as possible. He bristled at the thought of the medical marijuana movement turning into a business driven by the bottom line. "Taxes?" he erupted in a San Francisco café in December 2009. "We shouldn't pay taxes. The government should pay us reparations for all the lives they've ruined."

Peron even recorded a video denouncing the initiative and posted it on YouTube. In it, he took aim at what he called the excessive restrictions in Lee's initiative. "To deny 18-year-olds is wrong. They can go buy cigarettes, they can go kill for our country . . ." Peron said in his rapid-fire style. "I started smoking when I was 18, and it saved my life. Also, a five-by-five area is too small. We need the Central Valley." Peron criticized Lee for leading the medical marijuana movement into the cold world of finance. "We've given too much power to one man, to a person who has no sense of destiny, no sense of what it is to have power. He has money, and he equates that money with power," Peron said. "My power came from my heart and my friends. This is a movement about people, not money."

Peron said it was awkward to speak out against the initiative, but he felt he had no choice. "I don't like war, and I hate civil war. War with my friends is wrong," Peron said into the camera. "But I'm prepared for war. To sit back and do nothing would be wrong."[13] Although Lee described Peron at a 2008 NORML conference as one of his heroes and the godfather of the medical marijuana industry, the split between the two men over the initiative was such that Peron stopped teaching at Oaksterdam.

Don Duncan, the California director of the ASA, declined to take a position on the initiative because the organization's charter prevented it from endorsing political campaigns. But he said medical cannabis patients must be included in the dialogue as more states considered legalizing adult use. "Medical marijuana is not a means to an end; it's a means unto itself. What's not useful is for people to pretend to be medical marijuana advocates when they have a different agenda in mind. There's no integrity to that," Duncan said. "What could happen is it could be hurtful to our cause because it will be seen as a bait and switch. Advocacy for medical use and patients' rights should not be seen as a stalking horse. It's important that activists identify which side they're on and stick to their message."

Lee brushed off the criticisms. As in other rights movements, Lee said, many see no need to keep pushing once they become comfortable. "I've seen a lot of people in the industry who have a monopoly. They're making millions of dollars, and they see legalization as a threat," Lee said. "There's a comfort level with the way things are. They're making lots of money; they have lots of good bud, so why rock the boat?"[14] But Lee is still driven to change the status quo. He said that relentless forward movement has accomplished much for the medical cannabis industry, and it would be dangerous to stop when so much was still left to do. "That's what has caused things to move forward: people who took action through civil disobedience, opening dispensaries, and saying, 'We are going to provide the sick with medicine, and if you want to bust us, prosecute us, imprison us, come ahead,'" Lee said. "If the movement followed those who said 'We'll just wait for the laws to change,' the laws would never change. It never works." By pushing ahead against the advice of other industry leaders, Lee was prodding a reluctant movement toward legalization—the original goal of marijuana activists dating back to the 1960s.

The tension noted by Lee has its counterparts in other movements. In the 1970s gay rights movement in San Francisco, for example, the Alice B. Toklas Democratic Club refused to endorse firebrand Harvey Milk in his failed campaigns for San Francisco supervisor and state assemblyman. Milk and other like-minded activists broke off to form the more pugnacious San Francisco Gay Democratic Club. Another example is suffragist Alice Paul and other activists who split from the established National American Woman Suffrage Association during the First World War, when they thought the organization's leader was more concerned about cultivating influence with President Wilson than with winning the vote for women. Paul cofounded the National Woman's Party (NWP), which actively campaigned against Wilson and other incumbent Democrats who refused to publicly endorse the Nineteenth Amendment.

Lee downplayed any comparison between himself and these earlier activists, but he said the movement to legalize cannabis was urgent. Since 1995, there have been 9.5 million arrests for marijuana in the United States, and 41,000 Americans are currently in state or federal prison on marijuana charges. Lee said each of those prisoners unnecessarily represents a fractured family, a disrupted career, and possibly a ruined life.

The Loyal Opposition

In January 2010, spectators were still squeezing into a meeting room in the California State Capitol as San Francisco assemblyman Tom Ammiano gaveled the Public Safety Committee to order. Ammiano welcomed the overflowing crowd with a big smile and promised an exciting agenda.

The committee was going to discuss Ammiano's bill, which was the first ever that sought to legalize, regulate, and tax marijuana. It was similar to Richard Lee's initiative with one important difference: no one thought it had a chance. Despite marijuana's high approval rating in California, elected officials were still worried that voting for its legalization made them vulnerable to an opponent's charge of being weak on crime or morally deficient. But even with the poor prognosis, Ammiano looked pleased, leading some reporters to wonder whether he had wrangled enough votes to at least pass the bill through the seven-member committee.

Despite AB 390's poor chances, a coalition of California law enforcement and religious leaders were alarmed: so alarmed, in fact, they organized a joint appearance at the committee meeting to oppose the bill. Bishop Ron Allen, the founder and president of the International Faith-Based Coalition, led the pastors and church members; San Mateo Police Chief Susan Manheimer, president of the California Police Chiefs Association, led the law enforcement associations, which included the state Narcotics Officers Association, the District Attorneys Association, and the California State Sheriffs Association.

In the packed meeting room, 16 city police chiefs sat stiffly in their dress blues while representatives of the Marijuana Policy Project and the Drug Policy Alliance argued that law enforcement agencies had failed miserably in enforcing anti-marijuana laws. Despite 78,400 marijuana arrests in 2008, mostly for possession of small amounts, marijuana was still readily available on street corners and schoolyards. "Most voters overwhelmingly know that prohibition has failed," said Aaron Smith, California policy director for the Marijuana Policy Project. "Prohibition has failed to stop or curb marijuana availability."[15]

When their turn came, the bill's opponents told the committee legalization would increase marijuana use, which in turn would increase violent crime, drug dependency, and other health problems. Bishop Allen said he had buried six youths in the low-income Sacramento community where he ministers because of drug abuse. If marijuana were made legal, he expected to bury many more. Two police chiefs told the committee that problems caused by marijuana use would strain public safety resources. Dr. Andrea Barthwell, a former White House deputy drug czar under President George W. Bush, flew in from Illinois, where she is respected for her work in drug treatment. Barthwell told the committee its vote would reach far beyond the borders of California.

"The eyes of America are on you. We've taken California's lead on a number of health trends. You Californians have taught us how to eat healthy, control exposure to secondhand smoke, limit emissions from vehicles, and give pedestrians the right of way," she said. "However, today you contemplate making marijuana legal with a flawed scheme to tax and regulate it, a scheme that will benefit drug cartel kingpins and street corner dealers while it increases the burden of public safety systems, creates chaos in the healthcare delivery system, and devastates the public health system of California."[16]

The committee approved the bill by a four-to-three vote. In a press conference afterward, Ammiano said he would continue to push his bill even though Lee's initiative stood a much better chance of winning. "The state government and the state legislature are going to need to exercise control once that initiative passes," he told reporters. "I view today as a very, very important step in that process. Today demonstrated that [assembly members] are now willing to say this is worthy of discussion, when before the subject was met with silence, and legislators would avoid any discussion of the issue."[17]

The same coalition of law enforcement agencies planned to challenge Lee's initiative, and their testimony hinted at their larger strategy. They will likely argue legalization would have a devastating effect on the state's public health and safety. There would be a significant rise in organized crime, violence, cancer, addiction, dropout rates, and traffic deaths. Although those arguments were likely to carry weight, they seemed to ignore the fact that marijuana has been widely used in the state for decades, and they had failed to produce statistics to back up their claims. For example, there were 1,489 alcohol-related traffic fatalities in California in 2007, according to the Department of Motor Vehicles (DMV).[18] But the DMV kept no such data on marijuana-related traffic fatalities. Instead, marijuana was lumped in with other drugs under the general heading of drug fatalities, which numbered 749 that year.

Similarly, there are conflicting studies on marijuana as a major health threat. For example, the National Institutes of Health's 2006 study claimed there was next to no risk of cancer, no matter how much or how long marijuana was smoked. But a 2008 study by New Zealand scientists determined that smoking one joint was equivalent to smoking 20 cigarettes; they warned of a pending "epidemic" of lung cancer. Marijuana smoke is on California's list of chemicals known to the state to cause cancer or reproductive toxicity, but marijuana itself is not. Although most users prefer to smoke marijuana, it can also be ingested through edible goods and vaporizers, which pose no risk to the lungs. Neither marijuana nor marijuana smoke is on the U.S. Department of Health and Human Services list of carcinogens. And despite decades of heavy use in the United States, there is no official estimate of health costs associated with marijuana.[19]

Even so, law enforcement agencies argue that marijuana is dangerous. In the hall after the Public Safety Committee passed Ammiano's bill, police chief Scott Kirkland shook his head and smiled ironically. Tall, ruggedly handsome, and easygoing, Kirkland was on the board of California Police Chiefs Association and chaired its Medical Marijuana Task Force. Kirkland broadened his smile, shook his head again, and had only one comment: "Damn politics." Then he walked away with a group of fellow police chiefs.

Kirkland's primary reason for opposing legalization was its effect on children and youth. There was already too much marijuana in schools, and since medical marijuana had become legal, the situation had deteriorated. If adult use were legalized, he feared it would grow into an even bigger problem. In California, high school students who turned 18 before graduation could obtain medical cannabis recommendations, and many had become marijuana mules for their underage classmates. "Some of these students turn into de facto high school drug dealers not because they're prone to it, but just because they turn 18," Kirkland said. He had received calls from parents who found a bag of weed in the family car after their teenager had been driving it. "The parents want us to come and arrest them, or at least give their kid a scare, and I have to tell them I can't do it because their son or daughter has a medical marijuana recommendation, and it's legal for them to have marijuana," Kirkland said.[20]

Kirkland was worried about medical reports that marijuana use could slow brain development, particularly among male teenagers. Kirkland said he was no expert, but he suspected a correlation between the higher THC content in marijuana and higher rates of learning disabilities among American teenagers. And like many marijuana activists, he was frustrated that the Controlled Substances Act had stymied federal spending on research because marijuana was a Schedule I narcotic. He particularly wanted to see more medical research into marijuana's effect on children. "I could give a rat's ass about the 50-year-old guy who wants to smoke a joint in his house," Kirkland said. "If that's how he gets relief from societal woes, so be it."

As for the legalization campaign, Kirkland said proponents had touted exaggerated estimates for the industry's potential tax revenues. When the state Board of Equalization analyzed Ammiano's legalization bill for potential revenue, it estimated the entire marijuana industry, both medical marijuana and the black market, was worth about $14 billion a year in California. That meant the state could collect roughly $1.3 billion in annual revenue if the bill passed. But when Kirkland looked into how the Board of Equalization came up with those numbers, he was stunned. The board had relied on a production report written by Jon Gettman, a former president of NORML and a regular contributor to *High Times* magazine. "Gettman's estimates are hogwash," Kirkland said. "They're more than double any law enforcement estimates."

Kirkland was right that the estimates were tricky, largely because of the secretive nature of the industry. Gettman based his estimate on the total weight of plants seized by the DEA and U.S. Customs and Border Protection in a particular year. His critics argued that applying the supply-side method was flawed because DEA agents inflated their seizure numbers to justify the cost of their eradication program. Harvard economist Jeffrey Miron, perhaps the most respected authority on the economics of drug use, had applied a demand-based model to estimate the value of the marijuana market. Extrapolating from marijuana use surveys conducted by U.S. Department of Health and Human Services and considering the current price per gram, Miron estimated the entire U.S. marijuana market to be around $14 billion—the same figure Gettman had attributed to California alone.

Kirkland didn't know which figure was more accurate, but he was alarmed how quickly the media, with apparently little analysis, seized on Gettman's numbers. Another contested statistic was the number of marijuana arrests. The proponents usually cited 75,000 such arrests each year in California. That number was accurate, Kirkland said, but in California, possession of one ounce or less was punishable by a maximum fine of $100. "They're arrests, but they're transitory arrests, which means they get a ticket and go on their way," Kirkland said. "But if you read the newspapers, it sounds like we spend all our time looking for people who have small amounts of marijuana on them so we can lock 'em up. Believe me—we have other things to do."

Kirkland also criticized the overall tenor of the media coverage, which he felt favored the cannabis industry. "I'll talk to a reporter for up to an hour, and when the stories come out, I'll have one sentence, and Richard Lee will have three paragraphs,"

Kirkland said. In 2009, Kirkland sent an editorial to the *Sacramento Bee*, one of the state's most respected newspapers, after it ran a prolegalization piece by Aaron Smith, the policy director for the Marijuana Policy Project, who cited Gettman's tax revenue projections. Kirkland respectfully challenged Smith's assertions, but the *Bee* declined to run his piece. It finally appeared in the lower-circulation *Stanislaus County Insider*.[21]

Some police chiefs are frustrated by top law enforcement officials who are reluctant to publicly oppose legalization. Kirkland said he attributed that reluctance to the shaky job security of most police chiefs. "One reason is age; a lot of police officers are near retirement age when they're made chief. Another is they can't survive problems in their own department, and the third is they can't survive the political climate of the city they work for," he said. "Too many chiefs are afraid to say anything because it might affect their job security. The same goes for elected officials."

Despite these challenges, Kirkland said he was confident voters would see through campaign rhetoric and realize legalizing yet another mind-altering drug was a bad idea. But convincing voters is a difficult task. It requires an ability to communicate strategically and an understanding of public opinion and its vagaries. Opponents found those qualities in longtime Sacramento lobbyist John Lovell, a former troubleshooter for Gallo Winery.

Lovell's disheveled, avuncular image belies his reputation as a shrewd political operator. In 2008, he managed the campaign to defeat Proposition 5, which would have required the state to create more drug rehabilitation programs and limited the court's authority to sentence nonviolent drug offenders to prison. Initially, Proposition 5 had a great deal of momentum. Early polling showed voters favored the proposition two to one, and wealthy pro-legalization tycoons contributed generously, including $1.4 million each from international financier George Soros and Jacob Goldfield, the former chief investment of Soros Fund Management. Proponents ultimately outspent the opposition $7.6 million to $2.9 million.[22]

But that was before Lovell went to work. He landed endorsements from U.S. senators Dianne Feinstein and Barbara Boxer as well as California attorney general Jerry Brown, actor Martin Sheen, and farmworker icon Dolores Huerta. Lovell's campaign hammered home the view that the initiative was a "get-out-of-jail-free card" for drug offenders. "All defendants had to do was claim drug addiction, and the prosecutor would have the burden of proving otherwise. Voters didn't like that," Lovell said. "We won the election with 59 percent of voters saying no compared to 40 percent saying yes. It was a remarkable turnaround."

Two years after the defeat of Proposition 5, law enforcement again turned to Lovell. Several police associations, including the California Police Chiefs Association and the California Narcotics Officers Association, were working with Lovell to shape their campaign. Lovell said he was confident the initiative would fail. There were a number of flaws in its text that he said would be relatively easy to exploit. "I think the authors made the classic blunder of having too many proponents in the room when they wrote it, and there was no one to thoroughly challenge some of its provisions."

Lovell said the initiative gave a false impression of how much tax revenue it would raise and allowed cities and counties to regulate the cannabis industry as each saw fit. "It will create 500 marijuana nations, and it will be one big race to the bottom,"

Lovell said. "Mexican and Asian drug cartels won't disappear; they'll just set up shop in friendly cities and towns and continue to operate with impunity." The rules would change every time law enforcement officials crossed a city or county line in what Lovell described as a "confusing crazy quilt of laws, regulations, and policies." The initiative would also create problems for businesses, which couldn't fire anyone for testing positive for marijuana. Instead, employers would have to demonstrate that the worker was impaired. Because federal contracts include a drug-free clause, California businesses could also miss out on lucrative opportunities.

Both campaigns were planning no-holds-barred strategies. Polls favored legalization, but that was no guarantee. One thing was certain; the campaign would be watched more closely than any other state initiative in the country. Its passage would send a clear signal to government officials and politicians throughout the country.

The initiative's success would also mean a great deal of change for the medical marijuana industry. Smaller dispensaries, which have had the market entirely to themselves for years, could face stiff competition from well-funded and business-savvy investors. Unencumbered by Proposition 215's not-for-profit requirements, they could capture market share by undercutting prices, launching aggressive advertising campaigns, or using political influence to squeeze small operators out of the marketplace. Franchises could eventually spread to Oregon, Washington, and Nevada, which were also developing campaigns to legalize adult use.

But even if the legalization initiative failed, the marijuana industry would continue to grow at a rapid clip. In Colorado the industry was quickly catching up to California in the number of dispensaries, political sophistication, and support infrastructure. Maine, Rhode Island, New Mexico, and Montana were developing successful dispensary models. Insiders joked about the rise of "Starbuds"—a fictional corporate-styled dispensary chain with identical interior designs, uniformed budtenders, and standardized customer greetings—but that reality might not be far off.

No matter what the vehicle—legalization or the continued growth of the medical marijuana industry—the marijuana business would continue to change rapidly. And in the misty, forested hills of northern California, longtime marijuana-growing communities were watching the new developments anxiously—and wondering whether their way of life would soon be finished.

CHAPTER 9

Heartland

If the Bay Area is the political center of California's marijuana industry and Los Angeles is its financial engine, the Emerald Triangle is its agricultural heartland. Consisting of three connecting counties (Humboldt, Mendocino, and Trinity) in northern California, the region's landscape is breathtaking. In Humboldt County, which is internationally associated with marijuana growing, massive redwood trees in the lower hills look like they sprang off the pages of a science fiction novel, and the rugged Lost Coast is the longest stretch of undeveloped beach in the West. Forested hills sweep upward from the edge of the Pacific Ocean and roll eastward from ridge to valley to summit. In fact, 80 percent of Humboldt County's 4,052 square miles is undeveloped forestlands, rangelands, and protected parklands.

Despite Humboldt County's natural beauty, its economic viability has always been tenuous. For generations, locals relied on the fishing and timber industries. But overfishing and logging-related habitat contamination ruined the fishing industry, and unbridled corporate timber cutting in the 1980s and 1990s felled some of the oldest and tallest trees on earth and nearly exhausted the timberlands that had sustained logging jobs for more than 100 years.

As those industries failed, another was quietly taking root. Humboldt's remote hill country turned out to be an almost ideal place to grow marijuana, and by the late 1970s, its cultivation had become an important part of the regional economy. By the 1990s, the Emerald Triangle was providing California with most of its weed. Land prices soared as wannabe marijuana millionaires flocked to the region to buy land on which they could plant their own crops, or lease to more experienced growers. Over time, the Emerald Triangle came to depend on marijuana—and its high market value.

When the Control and Tax initiative was certified for the ballot, it struck fear into the hearts of many growers who worried legalization would lower prices. Still worse, some speculated large companies would undercut prices with vast fields of marijuana grown on massive legal farms. Humboldt County residents have leaned toward libertarianism and a general mistrust of government for decades. And growers, tempered by decades of DEA raids, have even stronger antigovernment sentiments. Nonetheless some growers talked about organizing an antilegalization campaign. The slogan "Save Humboldt County, Keep Pot Illegal," started turning up on bumper stickers, T-shirts, trucker hats, and refrigerator magnets. Their worry was understandable. In the last 20 years, the region had seen two major industries collapse. Marijuana, they said, could be next.

In the town of Arcata, it was not hard to see how the marijuana industry had permeated the culture. In some cases, it was obvious, like the medical marijuana dispensary just across the street from the town's historic plaza, or the constant smell of marijuana wafting through the hallways of the 90-year-old Hotel Arcata. Other indications were subtler though still tinged with the mystique of marijuana money. In a cozy Italian restaurant just off the plaza, a dinner party repeatedly ordered $100 bottles of wine three at a time. No one in the group looked older than 20, and the four males wore their camouflage baseball caps at the table. In the parking lot of the North Coast Co-op market, a young couple in Peruvian sweaters, their long blonde dreadlocks dangling from knitted headwear, climbed out of a Prius that still had the dealer sticker in the window.

It's impossible to gauge the size of Humboldt County's marijuana industry, but it's commonly thought to constitute between one-third and two-thirds of the county's $3.6 billion economy. About 30,000 people are estimated to be regularly involved in marijuana farming in some capacity. Marijuana had increased property values, sustained small businesses, and helped keep public agencies afloat. The industry was so robust that even three decades of raids by state and federal law enforcement agencies couldn't put a dent in production.

Kym Kemp starting writing about marijuana culture in Humboldt County in 2007. By 2010, she was considered an unofficial spokeswoman for growers, and the media frequently quoted her on issues facing the marijuana community. Kemp's family has lived in Humboldt and Mendocino counties since the 1850s, and her sensibilities are steeped in the area's history, lore, and customs. She came of age in the rural mountains of southern Humboldt County, where the industry first stirred to life, and she has been a close observer of marijuana farming as it grew into an economic powerhouse.

Humboldt County's marijuana saga began in the early 1970s,

when young hippies made the exodus from Haight-Ashbury and elsewhere. Uninterested in conventional urban and suburban lifestyles, and inspired in part by the writings of Henry David Thoreau as well as Bradford Angier's *At Home in the Woods* and *We Like It Wild*, the new residents helped form what would soon be called the "back-to-the-land" movement. Its members, whom the locals called "newcomers," thought they could move onto remote properties and live off chickens, a few cows, and vegetable gardens. But it was hard to feed a family from homegrown gardens, and there were also the costs of heating fuel, proper clothing, and vehicle maintenance. Some of the men looked the part of rugged mountain men with long hair, fringed buckskin shirts, and hunting knives in leather sheaths hanging from their belts. But more often than not, their girlfriends' or wives' welfare checks were feeding the family.

According to Kemp, part of the problem was that real estate agents took advantage of newcomers. For example, they showed them properties in April or May, when the creeks and streams were brimming with fresh water. Many newcomers didn't think to ask whether the water flowed throughout the summer. "If there's water in May, it probably won't be here in late June, and if it is, it for sure won't be there in August," Kemp said. "Then there were the winters. Some newcomers lived in tepees, or they would dig shelters in the ground like the Native Americans did, but the rains are relentless here in winter, and they would be washed out." Many newcomers gave up because their relationships didn't survive or they couldn't adapt to the rigors of rural life. Those who stuck it out usually had previous experience in farming or a job in town.

Others started growing and selling marijuana. Kemp remembered hearing about marijuana farms for the first time in 1972, when she was in the seventh grade. Later when she attended South Forks High School in the rural town of Miranda, talk about marijuana growing was common. The school, which had 350 students, served families from the deep backcountry. Some had to travel more than an hour on dirt roads to attend. Others lived so far away that their parents boarded them with families who lived closer to the school.

By the time Kemp was a junior, it was well known that certain kids were growing marijuana. "And it wasn't necessarily the newcomer kids, like you would have thought. It was the redneck kids, the back-ranchers, whose families lived in the hills for generations," Kemp said. "The adult rednecks and the hippies didn't like each other, but their kids got along, and that's how many of the redneck kids learned to grow. I'm still friends with most of them. They became expert growers and are still at it today, or their children are."

Kemp married Kevin Church in 1986, and they've raised their three boys in southern Humboldt. Church worked for Caltrans, the state department of transportation, as had Kemp's grandfather and father. Church's parents were newcomers, and even though he had lived in Humboldt County for nearly three decades, Kemp still thought of him as "not from here." They lived high in the hills above Garberville, a town of about 2,500 residents that has been called the Emerald Triangle's unofficial capital. The only other building they could see was a small white ranch house on the other side of a valley, and the only man-made noise was the occasional whir of a chainsaw.

Kemp wouldn't say whether she was ever a grower, and she didn't smoke pot. But some of her friends and family had been marijuana farmers, and the culture was an inseparable part of the rural area where she was born, raised, and made her home. She couldn't recall any utopian period when growers felt both prosperous and secure. The financial rewards of growing were great, but it had always been a rough trade. "In the 1970s, there wasn't a whole lot of money," she said. "By the 80s, the price of a pound went up to $1,200, and everyone was very excited. But then there were the murders that really shocked everybody." County sheriffs investigated nine marijuana-related murders during a one-year period beginning in October 1981. Chief of detectives Lt. Dennis Decarli fanned the flames, suggesting there were even more bodies buried in the backcountry.

Some of the murders were related to crop thefts. One was the shotgun killing of Forrest Clammer, a pot farmer who lived near Garberville. Friends and neighbors first noticed he was missing on Labor Day, but nobody notified the authorities until November. Deputies told the press his friends had waited to notify the sheriff's office because they didn't want officers snooping around before the October harvest. Police arrested David Sieber, who worked for Clammer, for the murder, though he was never convicted. At the time police claimed the motive was 100 or more plants that Sieber had allegedly run off with.[1]

Not long after that, an out-of-town roofer named Rene Palomino and his friend Armando Mendoza traveled to southern Humboldt on a stormy September night to steal marijuana crops. But when they couldn't find any farms, Palomino took Mendoza to the small home of Katherine Davis. According to Palomino, Mendoza broke into the house, dragged Davis downstairs, and demanded to know where her money was. Davis turned over $1,000 to Mendoza, who beat her to death.[2] Davis's daughter was a longtime friend of the Kemps, who later bought the Davis home.

As news of the murders spread through the region, growers realized they were in a dangerous business. Near harvest time, when crop theft was most likely to occur, some growers slept in their gardens with automatic rifles or machine guns. In backwoods areas and on public parklands, growers rigged their crops with crude booby traps made from rattraps and dangled fishhooks at eye-level from tree branches. Others patrolled their farms with attack dogs.

Just when paranoia about robberies was at its height, a new threat appeared. In 1983, California formed a new multi-agency task force called the Campaign Against Marijuana Planting (CAMP), whose sole objective was to eradicate illegal marijuana cultivation and trafficking in the state. Funded by the Reagan administration, the raids began almost immediately and continue today. Since 1983, CAMP's Web site claims the agency has seized 6.9 million plants. "They were relentless through the early 1990s," Kemp said. "But the worst was Operation Green Sweep."

In the summer of 1990, another joint task force under the leadership of the federal Bureau of Land Management (BLM) made a base camp in Humboldt County. The task force was made up of drug agents, California National Guardsmen, and 60 soldiers from the 7th Infantry Division. It was also the first time the U.S. military had been deployed against American citizens in that way. Green Sweep used Vietnam-style tactics during their raids in the Kings Range National Conservation Area. Blackhawk helicopters flew circles over raid areas while more than 200 troops, guardsmen, and agents blocked roads, interrogated residents, and prowled the woods with M-16 assault rifles.

That summer, Kemp encountered Operation Green Sweep firsthand while walking on a rural road. "Keep in mind this is a dirt road that you can walk on for an hour and probably never see anybody," Kemp said. "It was a beautiful summer day, and I was walking along barefoot in a white, hippie kind of dress. All of a sudden a soldier steps out of the woods and aims an assault rifle at me."

As the Green Sweep raids continued, Humboldt residents accompanied by the Garberville Marimba Band staged protests outside BLM headquarters. Residents filed a civil lawsuit demanding the military be prevented from participating in drug enforcement raids and that helicopters not buzz private homes from low altitudes. Some residents even took shots at the Blackhawks as they patrolled the mountain range. After two weeks, the operation was cut short for unexplained reasons, but residents said it was related to the protests, the lawsuit, and national press attention.[3]

Turning Inward

The raids did not slow marijuana cultivation or trafficking. But they did have a profound effect on the industry. The constant threat of arrest sent marijuana farms indoors where growing practices and marijuana itself would undergo dramatic changes.

Largely due to inventive amateurs in the Pacific Northwest, the quality of marijuana grown in the United States had improved greatly by the early 1980s. Outdoor growers crossbred two major strains, sativa and indica, and created robust hybrids that maintained each strain's desirable qualities: sativa's smoothness and "clear, bell high" and indica's higher potency and hardiness. The development of the new strains was heralded as "the great revolution" by respected marijuana botanists. Strains like Northern

Lights, Skunk #1, and Big Bud changed the United States' reputation for growing third-rate weed to producing some of the best marijuana in the world.

Indoor gardeners took a step further. Innovative growers discovered they could control the yield, plant height, and flowering by manipulating water, light, carbon dioxide levels, and heat. By 1990, indoor gardeners were producing stubby plants the size of fireplugs that yielded flowers the size of a fist. They had also strengthened marijuana's principle psychoactive compound, THC. Before the crossbreeding revolution, THC levels of U.S.-grown marijuana were 2 or 3 percent. By the early 1980s, the new strains were producing plants with levels as high as 15 percent. With the new indoor techniques, levels can now exceed 20 percent.

Indoor growers also discovered they could accelerate photosynthesis. They exposed the plants to blinding light 24 hours a day, and by changing from metal halide to sodium lights, which mimic the autumn sun, they induced flowering. The whole process, seed to flower, took only eight weeks instead of eight to nine months for outdoor plants. By 1987, the new techniques were brought together under the rubric of "Sea of Green," a garden of closely spaced plant clones that, in two months' time, could produce three pounds of high-grade marijuana in an area the size of a pool table. Once again, the humble weed had demonstrated its tenacity. Government programs to eradicate marijuana had led to a much stronger plant that could be grown anywhere in the world with a reliable supply of water and electricity.

Even so, Humboldt County was still the heartland. Just how many indoor grows were in the county was impossible to tell, but their presence left a distinctive trail. The *North Coast Journal,* the county's prize-winning alternative weekly newspaper, ran a story in March 2010 that compared Humboldt County's PG&E usage to the rest of the state. The story ran with charts that showed the county's average electricity usage rising above the state average beginning in 1996 when indoor grows became popular. By 2007, Humboldt residents were using 61 kilowatt-hours (kwh) more per capita than the average California resident. During the trial of one indoor grower, the prosecutor used PG&E records to determine the defendant had used 10,000 kwh per month, or about 20 times the average California home. The county's indoor farms were generating an estimated 20,000 metric tons of CO_2 that was being released into the atmosphere.[4]

Growers began converting rental homes into production sites at such a high rate that it created housing shortages in Garberville, Arcata, McKinleyville, and Trinidad. In some cases, indoor growers knocked out walls or otherwise damaged rented homes to increase grow space. Afraid to hire an electrician to rewire homes into a garden-friendly environment, they did the work themselves, which created fire hazards. And a rash of home-invasion robberies resulted in several well-publicized deaths.

Neighbors began complaining about grow houses to police and elected officials. In one case, a grow house was operating across the street from the home of a county superior court judge. Even though many of the indoor growers illegally produced far more plants than were allowed under local medical marijuana regulations, the sheriff could do little. Part of the problem was a lack of resources. Collecting evidence from a midsize grow house took three days and cost taxpayers about $5,000.

Second-generation Humboldt carpenter Wade Delashmutt discovered how intractable the problem was when Montana resident Robert Rivello moved into the house next door. Delashmutt and his wife soon noticed the distinctive skunky smell of weed coming from Rivello's house, which stood only a few feet from theirs. People with pit bulls would often arrive at Rivello's late at night in what Delashmutt described as gangster-style Cadillacs.

Delashmutt complained to the police, and when that went nowhere, he began regularly attending the Arcata City Council meetings to complain. Former mayor Harmony Groves was sympathetic, but the council could do little after passing the information to the police department. Two years later, the county drug task force raided Rivello's home and another one he owned in a different neighborhood. Officers seized 600 plants, 28 pounds of dried marijuana, $12,000 in cash, and an ounce of methamphetamine. "This guy came from out of state with this incredibly brazen attitude," Delashmutt said. "After two years, I was incredibly angry. If I had kids, I probably would have killed him."[5]

Tension among Humboldt's traditional outdoor growers and the new breed of indoor growers is philosophical in nature. The back-to-the-landers had gone into the hills to escape mainstream greed and capitalism. They sought a simpler life based on the principles of the 1960s counterculture. "When most of them first started growing pot, it was so they could buy their kids new jeans for school instead of getting them a pair at the Goodwill," Kemp said. But many of the back-to-the-landers prospered; some were living like gentleman farmers and wintering in Thailand or other sunny places. In keeping with their 1960s sensibilities, however, they remained environmentally conscious and eschewed ostentatious displays of wealth.

Kemp was reluctant to generalize about the differences between indoor and outdoor growers. In fact, some longtime outdoor growers have gone indoors to help meet steep mortgage payments. But some contrasts are evident, she said. In the hills, where outdoor growing has a long tradition, indoor farmers who grow in old barns, outbuildings, and empty homes are usually younger. They are known to race around the hills in four-wheel drive Toyota trucks, which cause some locals to call them the "Knights of Toyota." They frequently demonstrate an aggressive, flashy style, which publicly identifies them as moneyed growers. "There's a certain type of indoor grower who wants the biggest truck, the smallest girlfriend who has the biggest tits," Kemp said. "Outdoor growers look at indoor growers as greedheads, indoor cowboys. And there's a sense they are less ethical."

Outdoor growers often criticize indoor growers for the environmental damage they cause in the hills. Fire danger from poor wiring is a major concern during the dry summer months. Fuel trucks delivering diesel to grow houses cause damage to the dirt roads. Several fuel spills have fouled creeks and groundwater. Indoor growers often dump their fertilizer-saturated soil outdoors, causing algae blooms in the creeks. The heavy use of diesel fuel releases harmful particulate matter and carbons into the air.

Outdoor growers are also irked by the big money indoor growers make. "If you're an outdoor grower with a certain back-to-the-land attitude, it's hard to see these guys, who have such a negative impact on the environment, making more money," Kemp said. "But the indoor prices have been coming down. Anybody who knows, knows that outdoor [marijuana] may not be as strong, but it's the better pot. And it's what most of the dispensaries seem to want right now."

Nonetheless Kemp said indoor and outdoor growers have more

in common than not, and ultimately they got along. "I sometimes think that most of the differences are related to age," Kemp said. "Young people want the fast money of indoor growing, the way young people do. Older people are willing to take a little more time."

Out of the Hills

In 2007, Kemp began publishing her blog, "Redheaded Blackbelt, Humboldt, and Other Loves." At first, Kemp was unwilling to break the high-country code of never discussing the business with outsiders, so she never mentioned marijuana in her blog entries. "You're conditioned to not talk about these things at all. This is a culture where it is extremely rude to ask somebody what they do," Kemp said. "You don't even ask them where they live unless it's what watershed they live in."

But it soon became almost impossible to write about the county and not write about marijuana. Finally, she wrote a piece about driving down from her home on a fall evening. "It was getting close to harvest time, and I could smell all the marijuana smells, one strain here and another there. I love that smell. It's a bit magic, a little mysterious and a bit of outlaw that mingles with the smell of soil, flowers, trees . . . "

Kemp's husband Kevin broke in from across the room to add his impressions. "It's the smell of economic viability and independence."

Kemp did a lot of hand wringing over whether to post her story. When she finally did, the reaction was positive. She felt freed to write about the hardscrabble weed, one of the most powerful forces in her community. Mostly she wrote about the cultural aspect of the local marijuana farming industry. She commented on mainstream media coverage, harvest festivals, bud contests, and environmental issues. She wrote about trimmers, the seasonal workers who make good money during harvest by trimming plants. One story, "Money Laundering in Humboldt," was about a common sight in Garberville's Laundromat—hundred dollar bills rolling around in a dryer. "It happens a few times a year. Usually it's a young grower dude who like most young guys is not overly careful," Kemp said. "He forgets to check his pockets before washing his clothes. It usually stays in the pocket while it's in the washer. But during the dryer cycle, all of a sudden you can see $2,000 in hundreds spinning around through the glass."

One of Kemp's most popular stories, "Growing Up Green," was a series of interviews with young people who were raised in grower households. She wrote about tough and rarely discussed issues like parental drug use and whether children were inclined to become growers themselves. She also discussed the pressure on kids to keep secrets. The children learned to live with a powerful and constant presence that Kemp called "the unspokenness." Kids felt that if they confided in a friend or had a slip of the tongue at school, their families would be destroyed. In the story, Kemp described a grower's son who broke up with high school girlfriends if they asked too many questions about what his family did for a living. Another said he lived with a woman for two years before telling her what the family business was.

Recently Kemp has been writing about the economic gloom that pervaded the hills and valleys of southern Humboldt. During the medical marijuana "green rush," the number of growers in California and other states had increased. There was more product on the market, and the price for a pound of Humboldt's best weed dropped from $4,000 to $3,000. Many Humboldt growers resented the dispensaries for causing the price drop while continuing to retail marijuana for about $7,000 a pound.

The 2010 Control and Tax initiative only exacerbated worries about the market. The main concern was that a tsunami of marijuana would hit the market and push prices down to a few hundred dollars a pound. "People have been hearing that [tobacco giant] R.J. Reynolds bought property in Mendocino and near Ferndale in southern Humboldt," said Kemp, who doesn't credit the rumor. "But no one has been able to verify it. It's always somebody heard it from somebody, who knows another person who knows someone, etc." Not only were Humboldt's growers alarmed, but politicians and government officials were unofficially concerned a drop in pot prices could hurt tax revenues, which in turn could result in a loss of government jobs and the ability to deliver services.

In the winter of 2010, Anna Hamilton, a talk show host on local station KMUD-FM, fanned the region's worst economic fears about legalization. Hamilton organized a community meeting at the Garberville Rotary Club so that locals could discuss the issue. Her "What's After Pot?" forum attracted more than 150 people, including a county supervisor, business owners, and economic development consultants. The event marked the first time the traditionally secretive growers discussed their problems in front of the public and media. At the meeting, Hamilton warned of hard times. "The legalization of marijuana will be the single most devastating event in the long boom-and-bust economy of Northern California," she said. "We are going to be ruined."[6]

Kemp, who supported legalization for moral reasons, didn't share Hamilton's bleak outlook. But the two women agree on one thing: Humboldt growers would have to rethink their business to retain their competitive advantage. After the Garberville forum, growers and suppliers became more involved in public discussions, and the Humboldt Medical Marijuana Advisory Panel was formed. Its goal was to establish a working relationship with county government officials and form grower co-ops that will certify their marijuana has been grown organically.

For the first time, Humboldt County was talking about embracing its reputation as the spiritual homeland of pot. Humboldt's name recognition and history could become valuable marketing tools, and the prospect of legalization had them considering ways to use these tools. "Trying to re-brand us—ignoring the name recognition we already have—is like Hollywood wanting to be known as the palm tree capital," Kemp said. "Why ignore what we are already famous for in favor of what a few people recognize? That doesn't mean disregard other good commodities like grass-fed beef and beautiful coastlines, but these should be packaged with our marijuana status, not instead of it."

The Humboldt County Convention and Visitors Bureau jumped in with both feet. Executive director Tony Smithers was awash with ideas for capitalizing on Humboldt's reputation for marijuana growing, hippie sensibilities, and outlaw mystique. The county could target the large cohort of prosperous baby boomers—"a bulge in the snake," as Smithers called them—who might like to reexperience the countercultural lifestyles of their youth. Smithers also thought growers could brand the highly recognizable Humboldt name the same way the Champagne region of France has branded its famous beverage.

Resident Debbie Green suggested promoting Humboldt as the Napa Valley of weed. Visitors, for example, could book rooms at working farms that Green called "marijuanaries." Visitors could have an authentic growing experience by clipping their own buds while being regaled with swashbuckling tales of '60s rebels living behind the "Redwood Curtain," DEA raids with automatic weapons and helicopters, and narrow escapes into the hills.

Kemp was excited and hopeful about the region's future. She said she couldn't imagine life in Humboldt without the marijuana culture and its values. Pot farming has preserved a rural way of life in southern Humboldt that has all but disappeared in other parts of the country. Unlike many other small towns, Kemp said, Garberville is still authentic and has not turned into a sentimental parody of itself. "In so many rural places, the young people move out and the corporate chain stores move in," she said. "In Garberville, we don't have that. There are a couple of chain hardware stores, but mostly all the others are mom-and-pop owned. And mom and pop can afford to stay in business because of marijuana."

Kemp said she worried about losing the rural values that characterize her southern Humboldt community. She said growers might be criminals as far as the law is concerned, but most of them are hard working, family oriented, and community minded. They support the Garberville Volunteer Fire Department (which had recently purchased a brand new engine), a small school, road maintenance, and even the Garberville hospice. "It's mostly marijuana money that funds all of those things," Kemp said. "This is a community that steps up for its own, and I love them for that. We need to step forward now, or this culture of harvest festivals and strong community bonds might be gone. The people who have been there for each other might no longer be there anymore."

Many growers blamed the legalization of medical marijuana for destabilizing the cultivation economy. After all, it was medical marijuana that created the green rush of people who converted their garages to indoor gardens and flooded the market with marijuana. It was medical marijuana that had softened the public's perception of marijuana in general and set it on the path to legalization. Many growers claim Proposition 215 has been the worst thing to happen to the Emerald Triangle's growing industry. And they suspect legalization would only make things worse.

"Off the Grid"

Ironically, another person unhappy with the medical marijuana industry was the person who created it. Dennis Peron knew Humboldt growers blamed him for Proposition 215 and the rise of the medical marijuana industry. He joked that he never visits the Emerald Triangle without a Kevlar jacket. But he shared the growers' disappointment, albeit for different reasons. Peron said the compassionate spirit the industry sprang from had been overtaken by venality and commercialism.

I interviewed Peron in San Francisco in late December 2009. He was running a bed and breakfast out of his home, which he called the Castro Castle. Part inn, part political club, part community center, the three-story home was also a portal to a bygone era. A garage-door mural of Buddha with a green marijuana leaf on his third eye dominated the front of the building. The rest of the façade was painted like a fanciful river-stone castle.

The guest rooms were decorated in a 1960s bohemian theme with colorfully painted walls, Indian-print bed coverings, ethnic handwoven fabrics, and potted palms. The backyard was thick with trees and vegetation. Colorful prayer flags crisscrossed between the main house and a guest cottage at the back of the property. Most surfaces were painted with Day-Glo colors, and sometimes at night, Peron turned on a black light that ignited the backyard with iridescent greens, yellows, and oranges. "They can see us from the space shuttle," Peron said with an impish smile. "They say, 'See those crazy lights? That's Peron's place.'"

At a nearby café, Peron talked about his disdain for greed and his disappointment in the industry. The Control and Tax initiative, he said, ran counter to his vision for medical marijuana. Peron wanted marijuana to stay "off the grid," somewhere above government taxation and crass commercialism. Citing a common 1960s counterculture belief, Peron said marijuana has the unique ability to open minds and inspire a gentler way of life, a gentler society. Medical marijuana profits, Peron said, should serve the common good rather than enrich the few.

"There are people who have carved out a niche for themselves in the dispensary business, and they are forcing their friends, some of them sick people who really need it, to pay higher prices for marijuana, and that pisses me off," he said. "And what do they do with the money? Try to tax and regulate. They didn't do anything else but drive around in Mercedes-Benzes and Lamborghinis."

Peron opened the San Francisco Cannabis Club in 1994 to honor his lover Jonathan West, who had died of AIDS. Peron's vision was to provide medicinal marijuana to the seriously ill and return any profits to the community through acts of kindness and the pursuit of social justice. That was the model Peron envisioned for Proposition 215. "It was about empowering people, not exploiting them," Peron said.

Perhaps Peron was being naïve. Business interests have long been effective at co-opting the concepts and emblems of social movements for their marketing strategies. In his book *The Making of a Counter Culture,* Theodore Roszak writes, "It is the cultural experimentation of the young that often runs the worst risk of commercial verminization—and so having the force of its dissent dissipated."[7] There are many examples. Apple Computer used spiritual leader Mahatma Gandhi's stature as a humanitarian in their "think different" advertising campaign. Mega clothing company Gap Inc. used the image of counterculture icon Jack Kerouac to sell khakis. Swedish car company Volvo used a passage from Kerouac's seminal book *On the Road* to sell expensive cars.

The purer concepts of social and cultural movements are almost always corrupted to some degree. The commercialization of the marijuana movement, which happened to be based on a valuable commodity, was probably inevitable.

Nonetheless, Peron said he hoped the marijuana industry would return to its movement origins, or that a new, compassionate marijuana subculture would arise. Peron's friend Harvey Milk taught him hope should be nurtured at all costs. "When you don't have hope, you tend to give up, and when you give up, you become a slave," Peron said. "It was hope that made 215 happen. No one thought it could be done."

Peron looked out the café window as though he were composing a thought. After a while, he said quietly that he had lost a lover and many friends to AIDS. Sometimes he felt he didn't have friends anymore, only acquaintances. "And Harvey . . . There's not a day I don't think about Harvey Milk," he said.

But his sadness soon lifted. He talked about political projects he wanted to work on and some minor remodeling projects he planned for the Castro Castle. As we were leaving, he stopped to talk to the woman who worked at the café. "This guy is writing a book about medical marijuana," he told her cheerfully. Then he turned to me with an impish smile. "I'm going to be the hero, right?"

Notes

INTRODUCTION

1. Jeffrey Miron, "The Budgetary Implications of Drug Prohibition," Department of Economics, Harvard University (Feb. 2010). http://www .economics.harvard.edu/faculty/miron/files/budget_2010_Final.pdf.

CHAPTER 1: OUT OF THE SHADOWS

1. Gail Brager profile, UC Berkeley Engineering Department. http:// coe.berkeley.edu/news-center/publications/forefront/archive/forefront -spring-2008/features/a-breath-of-fresh-air-how-alumna-gail-brager -opened-the-workplace-to-a-natural-cool.

2. John Geluardi "Issue Opens Window to Council Debate," *Contra Costa Times,* (June 30, 2007). http://www.gaylemclaughlin.net/press -CCT_06-30-07.htm.

3. Richmond City Council meeting (Feb. 2, 2009). http://richmond .granicus.com/MediaPlayer.php?view_id=10&clip_id=2049.

4. Malcolm Maclachlan, "Ammiano offers bill to legalize, tax marijuana," *Capitol Weekly* (Feb. 2, 2009). http://www.capitolweekly .net/article.php?_c=xsnyxajuuwt6vm&issueId=xsnwlbcd0tt4%20ed &xid=xsol29u6c298w6.

5. Betty Yee, "Chairwoman Yee Supports Assembly Bill 390:

Marijuana Control, Regulation, and Education Act," State Board of Equalization quarterly e-newsletter (Jan. 2009). http://www.boe.ca.gov/members/. . . "yee/pdf/Vol_3%20issue_1.pdf.

6. Under federal law doctors cannot "prescribe." They can only recommend. This is a very important distinction.

7. 2004 American Association of Retired People survey. http://docs.google.com/viewer?a=v&q=cache:osv M_kDtUSQJ:www.safeaccessnow.org/downloads/AARP.medical_marijuana.pdf+medical+marijuana+users+gender+statistics&hl=en&gl=us&pid=bl&srcid=ADGEEShtWmOA0KSSItZ4ERa6Kuvb7F4L9jr9dBU5KdDE36x2nODzaYSDICgQykKgGtk7I5LjlojbKoiLqkdMVloqiWIZ8Fh0Bv4OMnrFLUlZQpGuc2zfIo4oTy4CwOfMkUzbVYhN-ntj&sig=AHIEtbQM3GLFS2pkRnffxu5HgBEW2YHetw.

8. ABC/Washington Post poll (Jan. 2010). http://abcnews.go.com/images/PollingUnit/1100a3MedicalMarijuana.pdf.

9. Gallup Poll (Nov. 2009). http://www.gallup.com/poll/123728/u.s.-support-legalizing-marijuana-reaches-new-high.aspx.

10 Katharine Q. Seelye, "Barack Obama, Asked About Drug History, Admits He Inhaled," *New York Times* (Oct. 24, 2006). http://www.nytimes.com/2006/10/24/world/americas/24iht-dems.3272493.html.

11. Americans for Safe Access. http://safeaccessnow.org/section.php?id=27.

12. The California Police Chiefs Association. http://www.californiapolicechiefs.org/nav_files/ marijuana_files/AgencyDocs.html.

13. Michael Backes, "Pesticides and Politics," *About Medical Marijuana* (Oct. 15, 2009). http://aboutmedicalmarijuana.com/2009/10/15/pesticides-and-politics/.

14. 2010 anti-marijuana rally, Sacramento, CA.

CHAPTER 2: DAMNATION

1. Sidney Lee, ed., *Dictionary of National Biography,* Vol. XLII (New York: Macmillan and Co., 1895), 310.

2. Martin Booth, *Cannabis: A History* (New York: Picador, 2003), 113.

3. George Andrews, *The Book of Grass: An Anthology on Indian Hemp* (New York: Grove Press, 1967), 11.

4. Horatio C. Wood and Robert M. Smith, eds., *Therapeutic Gazette,* Vol. 3 (Detroit & Philadelphia: George S. Davis, 1887), 226.

5. Tod Mikuriya, ed., *Excerpts from the Indian Hemp Commission Report* (San Francisco: Last Gasp, 1994), 6.

6. Booth, *Cannabis,* 176.

7. Ronald Hamowy, ed., *Dealing with Drugs: Consequences of Government Control* (Lexington, MA: Lexington Books, 1987), 20.

8. John Kaplan, *Marijuana, the New Prohibition* (New York: World, 1970), 96.

9. Stephen R. Kandall, *Substance and Shadow: Women and Addiction in the United States* (Cambridge, MA: Harvard University Press, 1999), 111.

10. Albert Harry Goldman, *Grass Roots: Marijuana in America Today* (New York: Harper & Row, 1979), 262.

11. Diana H. Fishbein and Susan E. Pease, *The Dynamics of Drug Abuse* (Boston: Allyn & Bacon, 1996), 19.

12. Booth, *Cannabis,* 245.

13. U.S. Department of Health and Human Services, Office of Applied Studies, "Initiation of Marijuana Use: Trends, Patterns, and Implications Report" (2008). http://www.oas.samhsa.gov/mjinitiation/chapter3.htm.

CHAPTER 3: REDEMPTION

1. Obituary–Leo Paoli, *San Francisco Chronicle* (Apr. 4, 1997). http://articles.sfgate.com/1997-04-07/news/17747994_1_marijuana-laws-drug-laws-california-marijuana-initiative.

2. Graeme Zielinski, "Activist Robert C. Randall Dies; Won Right to Medical Marijuana," *Washington Post* (June 8, 2001), B07.

3. Bruce Lambert, "Vincent Hallinan Is Dead," *New York Times* (Oct. 4, 1992). http://www.nytimes.com/1992/10/04/us/vincent-hallinan-is-dead-at-95-an-innovative-lawyer-with-flair.html.

4. Mary Rathbun and Dennis Peron, *Brownie Mary's Marijuana Cookbook and Dennis Peron's Recipe for Social Change* (Trail of Smoke Publishing Co., 1996).

5. Arnold S. Trebach, *Fatal Distraction: The War on Drugs in the Age of Islamic Terror* (Bloomington, IN: Unlimited Publishing, 2006), 223.

6. Telephone interview with Jeff Jones (Feb 2010).

7. Jim Herron Zamora, "Hallinan: A Man at Odds with Authority," *San Francisco Chronicle* (Dec. 10, 2003). http://articles.sfgate.com/2003-12-10/news/17520521_1_father-vincent-hallinan-campaign-office-murder-conviction.

8. Americans for Safe Access, "Medical Marijuana Dispensary Ban Lawsuit Argued in Appellate Court" (Sept. 22, 2009). http://www.safeaccessnow.org/article.php?id=5795.

9. Kim Skornogoski, "Medical marijuana boom raises questions across Montana," *Great Falls Tribune*. http://www.greatfallstribune.com/article/20100425/news01/4250304.

10. Marijuana Policy Project, "Granite Staters, Your Guide to the Candidates' Views on Medical Marijuana" (July 2, 2009). http://granitestaters.com/candidates/bill_richardson.html.

11. Congressional Research Service, "Medical Marijuana: Review and Analysis of Federal and State Policy" (July 27, 2009). http://www.mpp.org/assets/pdfs/library/CRS-MMJ-09.pdf.

12. "ASA 2009 Accomplishments." http://www.safeaccessnow.org/section.php?id=27.

13. CannabisClubNetwork (Mar. 25, 2009). http://www.youtube.com/watch?v=Pkl2Yzhd6E8.

CHAPTER 4: AN INDUSTRY TAKES SHAPE

1. Dale Gieringer, "The Decade of the Cannabis Club," *O'Shaughnessys*, Winter/Spring 2007. http://www.pcmd4u.org/OShaughnessys/Backgrounder_files/Winter-Spring_2007.pdf.

2. Henry K. Lee, "Pair Indicted in Pot Stores Case," *San Francisco Chronicle* (July 18, 2007). http://articles.sfgate.com/2007-07-18/bay

-area/17253798_1_marijuana-sales-compassionate-caregivers-yellow -house.

3. Gieringer, "The Cannabis Club," *O'Shaughnessys*, Winter/Spring 2007.

4. Ibid.

5. Medical Marijuana of America Web site. http://www.medical marijuanaofamerica.com/pows/incarcerated-now/260.html.

6 Interview with Richard Lee, Oakland (May 2010).

7. Rona Marech, "Medical Pot Patients Flock to Oaksterdam," *San Francisco Chronicle* (Aug. 10, 2003). http://articles.sfgate.com/2003-08 -10/news/17502648_1_medical-marijuana-marijuana-clubs-marijuana -program.

8. Ibid.

9. Ibid.

10. Interview with Rebecca Kaplan, Oakland (Dec. 2009).

11. Anne Ostrom, "Cannabis Club Debate Vigorous in S.F.," *Contra Costa Times* (Aug. 28, 2005). http://cannabisnews.com/news/21/ thread21068.shtml.

12. Tod Mikuriya et al., "Medical Marijuana in California, 1996– 2006," *O'Shaughnessys*, Winter/Spring 2007. http://www.pcmd4u.org/ OShaughnessys/Backgrounder_files/Winter-Spring_2007.pdf.

13. Telephone interview with Aaron Peskin (Nov. 2009).

14. Medical Cannabis Commission. http://www.ci.berkeley.ca.us/ ContentDisplay.aspx?id=31260.

15. Oaksterdam University Web site. http://www.oaksterdam university.com/facultyoakland.html#lee.

16. Ibid.

17. Smart Voter. http://www.smartvoter.org/2009/07/21/ca/alm/ meas/F/.

18. Peter Hecht, "The Conversation: As Medical Marijuana Dispensaries Proliferate, Some Argue That the State Should Get a Cut of the Action," *Sacramento Bee* (Jan. 10, 2010). http://www.sacbee.com/ 2010/01/10/2449110/the-conversation-as-medical-marijuana.html.

CHAPTER 5: GROWING PAINS

1. Matthew Philips, "The Wild West of Weed," *Newsweek* (Oct. 15, 2009). http://www.newsweek.com/id/217921.

2. Patrick Range McDonald and Christine Pelisek, "L.A.'s Medical–Weed Wars," *LA Weekly* (Nov. 26, 2009). http://www.laweekly.com/2009-11-26/news/l-a-39-s-medical-weed-wars/.

3. Booth, *Cannabis*, 212.

4. McDonald and Pelisek, "Weed Wars," *LA Weekly*.

5. Bita Neyestani, "City Hall Seven Refuse to Take Pay Cuts," *San Francisco Examiner* (Mar. 19, 2010). http://www.examiner.com/x-9449-LA-City-Hall-Examiner~y2010m3d19-City-Hall-Seven-refuse-to-take-pay-cuts.

6. Daniel Heimpel, "L.A.'s Reefer Revolution," *LA Weekly* (July 16, 2009). http://www.laweekly.com/2009-07-16/news/los-angeles-reefer-revolution/2.

7. John Hoeffel, "L.A.'s Medical Pot Dispensary Moratorium Leads to Boom Instead," *Los Angeles Times* (June 3, 2009). http://articles.latimes.com/2009/jun/03/local/me-medical-marijuana3?pg=3.

8. Daniel B. Wood, "Los Angeles Cuts Back on Medical Marijuana Dispensaries," *Christian Science Monitor* (June 7, 2010). http://www.csmonitor.com/USA/2010/0607/Los-Angeles-cuts-back-on-medical-marijuana-dispensaries.

9. California Police Chiefs Association, Fact Sheet: Medical Marijuana Facilities within the City of Los Angeles (Dec. 14, 2006). http://www.californiapolicechiefs.org/nav_files/marijuana_files/files/fact_sheet.pdf.

10. Noah Galuten, "New KFC Opens in Palms?" *LA Weekly* blog (Aug. 27, 2009).

11. Solomon Moore, "Los Angeles Prepares for Clash over Medical Marijuana," *New York Times* (Oct. 17, 2009). http://www.nytimes.com/2009/10/18/us/18enforce.html.

12. John Hoeffell, "Judge Rules L.A.'s Ban on New Medical Marijuana Dispensaries Is Invalid," *Los Angeles Times* (Oct. 20, 2009). http://articles.latimes.com/2009/oct/20/local/me-pot-moratorium20.

13. Sandy Banks, "Medical Pot Proposal Erases Compassion," *Los Angeles Times* (Sept. 26, 2009). http://mobile.latimes.com/inf/infomo ?view=page8&feed:a=latimes_1min&feed:c=topstories&feed:i=494 91178&nopaging=1.

14. Telephone interview with Paul Reznick (Feb. 2010).

15. Telephone interview with Don Duncan (Jan. 2010).

16. John Hoeffell, "Dispensary Operators Say L.A. Marijuana Ordinance Will Harm Patients," *Los Angeles Times* blog (Jan. 26, 2010). http://latimesblogs.latimes.com/lanow/2010/01/dispensary -operators-say-la-marijuana-ordinance-will-harm-patients.html?utm _source=feedburner&utm_medium=feed&utm_campaign=Feed%3A +lanowblog+(L.A.+Now)

17. Tony Barboza, "Medical Marijuana Advocates Sue Los Angeles," *Los Angeles Times* (Mar. 3, 2010). http://articles.latimes.com/2010/mar/ 03/local/la-me-medical-marijuana3-2010mar03.

18. Ibid.

CHAPTER 6: THE NEW PROFESSIONALS

1. Alicia A. Caldwell and Manuel Valdes, "Drug Gangs Taking over U.S. Public Lands," AP (Mar. 1, 2010). http://www.google.com/ hostednews/ap/article/ALeqM5gf_NuUKux5IdoINS4Ug3ZXatiJV gD9E64ET00.

2. Rone Tempest, "DEA Targets Larger Marijuana Dispensaries," *Los Angeles Times* (Jan. 1, 2007). http://articles.latimes.com/2007/ jan/01/local/me-potbusts1.

3. Ibid.

4. Ibid.

5. Modesto Police Department press release (Feb. 3, 2003). http:// www.ci.modesto.ca.us/newsroom/releases/police/detail.asp?id=384.

6. Luke Scarmazzo, Kraz-Business Man video. http://www.youtube .com/watch?v=E5niNz39Fco.

7. Collective Wellness Web site. http://www.collectivewellness.org/ d/node/7.

8. Greta Mart, "Passion at Root of Martinez Medical Cannabis Dispensary Quest" (Mar. 18, 2010). http://www.martinezgazette .com/news/story/i713/2010/03/18/passion-root-martinez-medical -marijuana-di.

9. Interview with Don Morgan, Oakland (Jan. 2010).

10. Interview with Dale Clare, Oakland (Dec. 2009).

11. Fox 11 News, "Trutanich Opposes Medical Marijuana." http:// www.youtube.com/watch?v=7AhNb75N8V4&feature=player_ embedded_dispensary_quest.

12. Bootie Cosgrove-Mather, "Potent Pesticides Used in Tobacco," AP (April 4, 2004). http://www.cbsnews.com/stories/2003/04/24/ tech/main550925.shtml.

13. John Hoeffel, "A Medical Marijuana Success Story," *Los Angeles Times* (Nov. 16, 2009). http://articles.latimes.com/2009/nov/16/local/ me-weho-marijuana16/2.

14. Ibid.

15. Richmond City Council Meeting (Dec. 15, 2009). http:// richmond.granicus.com/MediaPlayer.php?view_id=10&clip_id=2049.

16. Telephone interview with Michael Aberle (Jan. 2010).

17. Interview with Micah Daigle, San Francisco (Dec. 2009).

18. Cynthia Needham, "Brown, URI students play key role in R.I. marijuana debate," *Rhode Island News* (Sept. 29, 2009). http://www .projo.com/news/content/MEDICAL_MARIJUANA_RIPAC_09 -27-09_3GFQVE9_v15.32a7e9b.html.

19. "Derek Copp Sentenced to 18 Months Probation on Drug Charge," *Grand Rapids News* (Aug. 10, 2009). http://www.mlive.com/ news/grand-rapids/index.ssf/2009/08/derek_copp_sentenced_to_18 _mon.html.

20. Green Party Web site for Clifford Thornton. http://www.gp.org/ speakers/detail.php?ID=12.

21. Nadelmann speech at SSDP annual convention, San Francisco (March 2009).

CHAPTER 7: THE NEW POLITICIANS

1. Ann Harrison, "Smoking Competitors: How Mirkarimi Balanced 'Big Pot' and the Concerned Neighbors around SF Medical Marijuana Clubs," *San Francisco Bay Guardian* (Apr. 2008). http://www.sfbg.com/40/08/news_pot.html.

2. Interview with Rebecca Kaplan, Oakland (Dec. 2009).

3. "The Report of the National Commission on Marihuana and Drug Abuse," commissioned by President Richard M. Nixon (Mar. 1972). http://www.druglibrary.org/schaffer/library/studies/nc/ncmenu.htm.

4. Brian Hood, "New Jobs for Men in 2010," *Esquire* (Apr. 5, 2010). http://www.esquire.com/the-side/feature/best-jobs-for-men-040510 #ixzz0kcoZz6ah.

5. CannBe Web site home page (2010). http://harborside managementassociates.com/index.html.

CHAPTER 8: LEGALIZATION

1. Jesse McKinley, "Strategizing Legalization Pros and Cons," *New York Times* (Apr. 24, 2010). http://www.nytimes.com/2010/04/24/us/24potside.html.

2. Brian Braiker, "California: Odd Bedfellows in the Pro-Pot Ballot Initiative," ABC News (Apr. 5, 2010). http://abcnews.go.com/Business/californias-pro-pot-movements-strangebedfellows/story?id=10273152 &page=2.

3. Ibid.

4. Telephone interview with Aaron Houston (Feb. 2010).

5. Drug Policy Alliance. http://www.drugpolicy.org/news/press room/pressrelease/pr032410.cfm.

6. Robert Reuteman, "The Marijuana Lobby All Grown Up," CNBC (Apr. 20, 2010). http://www.cnbc.com/id/36179727/The _Marijuana_Lobby_All_Grown_Up.

7. Peter Hecht, "Bigger Is Better," *Sacramento Bee* (Apr. 14, 2010). http://www.sacbee.com/2010/04/14/2676819/bigger-is-better-for-pot -dispensaries.html.

8. Fred Gardner, "Reconciling Medical Pot Use and Legalization," *Counterpunch* (Oct. 5, 2009). http://www.counterpunch.org/gardner 10052009.html.

9. Roger Parloff, "How Marijuana Became Legal," *Fortune* (Sept. 11, 2009). http://money.cnn.com/2009/09/11magazines/fortune/medical _marijuana_legalizing.fortune.

10. Gardner, "Reconciling . . . Legalization," *Counterpunch*.

11. Daniela Perdomo, "The Best Chance Yet for Legalizing Marijuana," *Alternet* (Jan. 4, 2010). http://www.truthout.org/104093.

12. Telephone interview with Robert Raich (Apr. 2010).

13. Peron denounces Control and Tax 2010 on YouTube. http://www.youtube.com/watch?v=dLpHwDJDR-s.

14. Telephone interview with Richard Lee (April, 2010).

15. California Public Safety Committee meeting (Jan. 12, 2010). http://www.calchannel.com/channel/viewVideo/929.

16. Ibid.

17. Press conference, Sacramento (Jan. 2010).

18. DMV California DUI Fact Sheet 1997–2007. http://www.dmv .ca.gov/about/profile/rd/Internet%20DUI%20Facts%20Sheet_2009 .pdf.

19. Marc Kaufman, "Study Finds No Cancer-Marijuana Connection," *Washington Post* (May 26, 2006); "Cannabis Use and the Risk of Lung Cancer," *European Respiratory Journal* (Jan. 2008); California Office of Environmental Health Hazard Assessment list of carcinogens (Apr. 2, 2010); U.S. Department of Health and Human Services, 11th Report on Carcinogens. http://ntp.niehs.nih.gov/ntp/roc/toc11.html.

20. Interview with Chief Scott Kirkland, El Cerrito (Dec. 2010).

21. Scott C. Kirkland, "The Truth, and Nothing but the Truth," *Stanislaus County Insider* (2009). http://stancoinsider.com/stanco insider_142.htm.

22. Secretary of state campaign records. http://cal-access.ss.ca.gov/ Campaign/Measures/Detail.aspx?id=1303172&session=2007.

CHAPTER 9: HEARTLAND

1. Gioia Delberto, "While U.S. Farms Go Bust, Some Growers Cashing in on the Profit of Pot," *People* (May 10, 1982). http://www.people. com/people/archive/article/0,,20082098,00.html; UPI, "Marijuana Culture: Violence, Intimidation, and Murder Erupt in Prime California Area Where It's Grown," *Reading Eagle* (Nov. 6, 1983). http://news .google.com/newspapers?nid=1955&dat=19831106&id=zhoiAAAA IBAJ&sjid=aaYFAAAAIBAJ&pg=3974,3701420.

2. UPI, "Marijuana Culture," *Reading Eagle* (Nov. 6, 1983).

3. Katherine Bishop, "Military Takes Part in Drug Sweep," *New York Times* (Aug. 10, 1990). http://www.nytimes.com/1990/08/10/ us/military-takes-part-in-drug-sweep-and-reaps-criticism-and-a-lawsuit .html?pagewanted=1.

4. Peter Lehman and Peter Johnstone, "The Climate Killers Inside," *North Coast Journal* (Mar. 11, 2010). http://www.northcoastjournal .com/issues/2010/03/11/climate-killers-inside/.

5. Telephone interview with Wade Delashmutt (Feb. 2010).

6. Donna Tam "The Road to Marijuana Legalization: Community Pot Meeting Spurs Hope for Legitimate Industry," *Times Standard* (Mar. 27, 2010). http://www.times-standard.com/ci_14769550.

7. Theodore Roszak, *The Making of a Counter Culture* (Berkeley: University of California Press, 1969).

Index

About the Author

John Geluardi has worked as a political reporter for daily newspapers for 10 years. As a staff writer for *SF Weekly*, he wrote features on crime, local and national politics, and culture. The San Francisco Peninsula Press Club awarded him three first-place awards in 2008 for stories he wrote on vice-presidential candidate Matt Gonzalez, the legendary Caffe Trieste, and a series of San Francisco homicides that police attempted to falsely classify as suicides. He also won awards for a story he wrote about San Francisco supervisor Dan White, who killed Mayor George Moscone and fellow supervisor Harvey Milk in 1977.

Other Books from PoliPointPress

The Blue Pages: A Directory of Companies
Rated by Their Politics and Practices, 2nd edition
Helps consumers match their buying decisions with their political values by
listing the political contributions and business practices of over 1,000 companies. $12.95, PAPERBACK.

Sasha Abramsky, Breadline USA:
The Hidden Scandal of American Hunger and How to Fix It
Treats the increasing food insecurity crisis in America not only as a matter of
failed policies, but also as an issue of real human suffering. $23.95, CLOTH.

Rose Aguilar, Red Highways: A Liberal's Journey into the Heartland
Challenges red state stereotypes to reveal new strategies for progressives. $15.95,
PAPERBACK.

John Amato and David Neiwert, *Over the Cliff:*
How Obama's Election Drove the American Right Insane
A witty look at—and an explanation of—the far-right craziness that overtook
the conservative movement after Obama became president. $16.95, PAPERBACK.

Dean Baker, *False Profits: Recovering from the Bubble Economy*
Recounts the causes of the economic meltdown and offers a progressive program for rebuilding the economy and reforming the financial system and stim-
ulus programs. $15.95, PAPERBACK.

Dean Baker, *Plunder and Blunder:*
The Rise and Fall of the Bubble Economy
Chronicles the growth and collapse of the stock and housing bubbles and explains how policy blunders and greed led to the catastrophic—but completely
predictable—market meltdowns. $15.95, PAPERBACK.

Jeff Cohen, *Cable News Confidential:*
My Misadventures in Corporate Media
Offers a fast-paced romp through the three major cable news channels—Fox
CNN, and MSNBC—and delivers a serious message about their failure to
cover the most urgent issues of the day. $14.95, PAPERBACK.

Marjorie Cohn, *Cowboy Republic:*
Six Ways the Bush Gang Has Defied the Law
Shows how the executive branch under President Bush systematically defied
the law instead of enforcing it. $14.95, PAPERBACK.

Marjorie Cohn and Kathleen Gilberd, *Rules of Disengagement:*
The Politics and Honor of Military Dissent
Examines what U.S. military men and women have done—and what their families and others can do—to resist illegal wars, as well as military racism, sexual harassment, and denial of proper medical care. $14.95, PAPERBACK.

Joe Conason, *The Raw Deal: How the Bush Republicans Plan to Destroy*
Social Security and the Legacy of the New Deal
Reveals the well-financed and determined effort to undo the Social Security Act and other New Deal programs. $11.00, PAPERBACK.

Kevin Danaher, Shannon Biggs, and Jason Mark, *Building the Green*
Economy: Success Stories from the Grassroots
Shows how community groups, families, and individual citizens have protected their food and water, cleaned up their neighborhoods, and strengthened their local economies. $16.00, PAPERBACK.

Kevin Danaher and Alisa Gravitz, *The Green Festival Reader:*
Fresh Ideas from Agents of Change
Collects the best ideas and commentary from some of the most forward green thinkers of our time. $15.95, PAPERBACK.

Reese Erlich, *Conversations with Terrorists:*
Middle East Leaders on Politics, Violence, and Empire
Offers critical portraits of six Middle Eastern leaders, usually vilified as terrorists, to probe the U.S. war on terror and its media reception. $14.95, PAPERBACK.

Reese Erlich, *Dateline Havana:*
The Real Story of U.S. Policy and the Future of Cuba
Explores Cuba's strained relationship with the United States, the island nation's evolving culture and politics, and prospects for U.S.–Cuba policy with the departure of Fidel Castro. $22.95, HARDCOVER.

Reese Erlich, *The Iran Agenda:*
The Real Story of U.S. Policy and the Middle East Crisis
Explores the turbulent recent history between the two countries and how it has led to a showdown over nuclear technology. $14.95, PAPERBACK.

Todd Farley, *Making the Grades:*
My Misadventures in the Standardized Testing Industry
Exposes the folly of many large-scale educational assessments through an alternately edifying and hilarious first-hand account of life in the testing business. $16.95, PAPERBACK.

Steven Hill, *10 Steps to Repair American Democracy*
Identifies the key problems with American democracy, especially election practices, and proposes ten specific reforms to reinvigorate it. $11.00, PAPERBACK.

Jim Hunt, *They Said What?*
Astonishing Quotes on American Power, Democracy, and Dissent
Covering everything from squashing domestic dissent to stymieing equal representation, these quotes remind progressives exactly what they're up against. $12.95, PAPERBACK.

Michael Huttner and Jason Salzman, *50 Ways You Can Help Obama Change America*
Describes actions citizens can take to clean up the mess from the last administration, enact Obama's core campaign promises, and move the country forward. $12.95, PAPERBACK.

Helene Jorgensen, *Sick and Tired:*
How America's Health Care System Fails Its Patients
Recounts the author's struggle to receive proper treatment for Lyme disease and examines the inefficiencies and irrationalities that she discovered in America's health care system during that five-year odyssey. $16.95, PAPERBACK.

Markos Kounalakis and Peter Laufer, *Hope Is a Tattered Flag:*
Voices of Reason and Change for the Post-Bush Era
Gathers together the most listened-to politicos and pundits, activists and thinkers, to answer the question: what happens after Bush leaves office? $29.95, HARDCOVER; $16.95 PAPERBACK.

Yvonne Latty, *In Conflict:*
Iraq War Veterans Speak Out on Duty, Loss, and the Fight to Stay Alive
Features the unheard voices, extraordinary experiences, and personal photographs of a broad mix of Iraq War veterans, including Congressman Patrick Murphy, Tammy Duckworth, Kelly Daugherty, and Camilo Mejia. $24.00, HARDCOVER.

Phillip Longman, *Best Care Anywhere:*
Why VA Health Care Is Better Than Yours, **2nd edition**
Shows how the turnaround at the long-maligned VA hospitals provides a blueprint for salvaging America's expensive but troubled health care system. $15.95, PAPERBACK.

Phillip Longman and Ray Boshara, *The Next Progressive Era*
Provides a blueprint for a re-empowered progressive movement and describes its implications for families, work, health, food, and savings. $22.95, HARDCOVER.

Marcia and Thomas Mitchell, *The Spy Who Tried to Stop a War:*
Katharine Gun and the Secret Plot to Sanction the Iraq Invasion
Describes a covert operation to secure UN authorization for the Iraq war and
the furor that erupted when a young British spy leaked it. $23.95, HARDCOVER.

Markos Moulitsas, *The American Taliban:*
How War, Sex, Sin, and Power Bind Jihadists and the Radical Right
Highlights how American conservatives are indistinguishable from Islamic
radicals except in the name of their god. $15.95, PAPERBACK.

Susan Mulcahy, ed., *Why I'm a Democrat*
Explores the values and passions that make a diverse group of Americans proud
to be Democrats. $14.95, PAPERBACK.

David Neiwert, *The Eliminationists:*
How Hate Talk Radicalized the American Right
Argues that the conservative movement's alliances with far-right extremists
have not only pushed the movement's agenda to the right, but also have be-
come a malignant influence increasingly reflected in political discourse. $16.95,
PAPERBACK.

Christine Pelosi, *Campaign Boot Camp:*
Basic Training for Future Leaders
Offers a seven-step guide for successful campaigns and causes at all levels of
government. $15.95, PAPERBACK.

William Rivers Pitt, *House of Ill Repute:*
Reflections on War, Lies, and America's Ravaged Reputation
Skewers the Bush Administration for its reckless invasions, warrantless wire-
taps, lethally incompetent response to Hurricane Katrina, and other scandals
and blunders. $16.00, PAPERBACK.

Sarah Posner, *God's Profits:*
Faith, Fraud, and the Republican Crusade for Values Voters
Examines corrupt televangelists' ties to the Republican Party and unprec-
edented access to the Bush White House. $19.95, HARDCOVER.

Nomi Prins, *Jacked: How "Conservatives" Are Picking Your Pocket—*
Whether You Voted for Them or Not
Describes how the "conservative" agenda has affected your wallet, skewed
national priorities, and diminished America—but not the American spirit.
$12.00, PAPERBACK.

Cliff Schecter, *The Real McCain: Why Conservatives Don't Trust Him—And Why Independents Shouldn't*
Explores the gap between the public persona of John McCain and the reality of this would-be president. $14.95, HARDCOVER.

Norman Solomon, *Made Love, Got War:*
Close Encounters with America's Warfare State
Traces five decades of American militarism and the media's all-too-frequent failure to challenge it. $24.95, HARDCOVER.

John Sperling et al., *The Great Divide: Retro vs. Metro America*
Explains how and why our nation is so bitterly divided into what the authors call Retro and Metro America. $19.95, PAPERBACK.

Mark Sumner, *The Evolution of Everything:*
How Selection Shapes Culture, Commerce, and Nature
Shows how Darwin's theory of evolution has been misapplied—and why a more nuanced reading of that work helps us understand a wide range of social and economic activity as well as the natural world. $15.95, PAPERBACK.

Daniel Weintraub, *Party of One:*
Arnold Schwarzenegger and the Rise of the Independent Voter
Explains how Schwarzenegger found favor with independent voters, whose support has been critical to his success, and suggests that his bipartisan approach represents the future of American politics. $19.95, HARDCOVER.

Curtis White, *The Barbaric Heart: Faith, Money, and the Crisis of Nature*
Argues that the solution to the present environmental crisis may come from an unexpected quarter: the arts, religion, and the realm of the moral imagination. $16.95, PAPERBACK.

Curtis White, *The Spirit of Disobedience: Resisting the Charms*
of Fake Politics, Mindless Consumption, and the Culture of Total Work
Debunks the notion that liberalism has no need for spirituality and describes a "middle way" through our red state/blue state political impasse. Includes three powerful interviews with John DeGraaf, James Howard Kunstler, and Michael Ableman. $24.00, HARDCOVER.

For more information, please visit www.p3books.com.

About This Book

This book is printed on Cascade Enviro100 Print paper. It contains 100 percent post-consumer fiber and is certified EcoLogo, Processed Chlorine Free, and FSC Recycled. For each ton used instead of virgin paper, we:

- Save the equivalent of 17 trees
- Reduce air emissions by 2,098 pounds
- Reduce solid waste by 1,081 pounds
- Reduce the water used by 10,196 gallons
- Reduce suspended particles in the water by 6.9 pounds.

This paper is manufactured using biogas energy, reducing natural gas consumption by 2,748 cubic feet per ton of paper produced.

The book's printer, Malloy Incorporated, works with paper mills that are environmentally responsible, that do not source fiber from endangered forests, and that are third-party certified. Malloy prints with soy and vegetable based inks, and over 98 percent of the solid material they discard is recycled. Their water emissions are entirely safe for disposal into their municipal sanitary sewer system, and they work with the Michigan Department of Environmental Quality to ensure that their air emissions meet all environmental standards.

The Michigan Department of Environmental Quality has recognized Malloy as a Great Printer for their compliance with environmental regulations, written environmental policy, pollution prevention efforts, and pledge to share best practices with other printers. Their county Department of Planning and Environment has designated them a Waste Knot Partner for their waste prevention and recycling programs.